2015 Edition

The practical guide to Health Care Advance Directives

Jo Kline Cebuhar, J.D.

2015 Edition

**The practical guide to
Health Care
Advance Directives**

by

Jo Kline Cebuhar, J.D.

Published in the United States of America by
Murphy Publishing, LLC
West Des Moines, Iowa

ISBN Print Edition: 978-0692432129

www.JoKlineCebuhar.com

Other books by Jo Kline Cebuhar, J.D.

EXIT – A novel about dying

SO GROWS THE TREE
Creating an Ethical Will
The legacy of your beliefs and values,
life lessons and hopes for the future

The Workshop Edition of
SO GROWS THE TREE
Creating an Ethical Will
The legacy of your beliefs and values,
life lessons and hopes for the future

Whose big idea was that?
Lessons in giving from the
pioneers of value-inspired philanthropy

Last things first, just in case...
The practical guide to Living Wills
and Durable Powers of Attorney for Health Care
Winner - USA Book News 2007 Best Book Awards
Finalist - ForeWard Magazine's 2007 Book of the Year

Principles
of Tax-deferred Exchanging
(1996 and 2001 editions)

Table of Contents

Why a 2015 Edition?

I wrote the first edition of this book, *Last things first, just in case . . . The practical guide to Living Wills and Durable Powers of Attorney for Health Care*, in 2006. What's changed since then? Well, let's see. Ten thousand Baby Boomers now qualify for Medicare every day, there is a seemingly endless menu of life extending medical treatments to choose from and three more states have legalized physician-assisted suicide—with many others considering it. To name just a few.

That's the big picture. On the personal level, throughout this near decade since 2006, readers of *Last things first* have shared with me their stories about death and dying. There's a common theme: as the end of life approaches, they don't understand what dying will mean for their loved ones, and afterwards, they don't understand what just happened. I heard about the mother who died unexpectedly less than a day after going to hospice, about a family forced to argue with doctors to get adequate pain relief for their father, about a husband's unambiguous end-of-life wishes being willfully ignored by health care professionals. For each of these survivors, the frustrating circumstances surrounding the loss cause as much anger or guilt or just plain sadness as the loss itself. I asked myself if I could do more to give people the information they need.

I'll also admit that as nature's beautiful pageant unfolds in my own life and in the lives of my friends, I have personally been forced to confront some of the issues that accompany aging—and hone the fine art of disregarding others. And truthfully, over time I've discovered elements of the 2006 edition that might have confused readers, and far be it from me to add to the baffling aura that already surrounds the subject of death and dying.

Other projects naturally followed the 2006 edition. I learned even more about the ancient tradition of Ethical Wills, and I wrote three books about the meaning of "legacy." There's a bit of that contained here, and I hope it inspires you to discover more of what is truly important to you in the years, months, days and hours leading up to your life's end.

So, that's some of what's changed since 2006. What remains constant is that somehow, some day, each and every one of us will die. Few can say with certainty in what manner and exactly when that will come about, and that's why having effective and meaningful health care advance directives plays such an important role in preparing for the final chapter of life. Whether to ponder the choices you'll make for yourself, to fully groom another person to step in as your proxy or to prepare to be the best advocate you can be for someone else, it makes sense to take care of *last things first, just in case*, don't you agree?

Chapter One
Denial isn't just a river in Egypt

I never think of the future. It comes soon enough.
Albert Einstein

Leroy and Effie were married 67 years ago. He was—still is—the best looking guy she's ever laid eyes on; a picture of her in that sundress gets him through 18 months on the front lines in World War II. They have a son and a daughter and five grandchildren. If Leroy and Effie said it once, they said it a thousand times: they can't imagine life without each other.

Then one day, without any warning whatsoever, Effie collapses on the bathroom floor. Leroy calls 9-1-1. In the emergency room, the admitting clerk asks Leroy if Effie has a Living Will. Leroy says he doesn't think so, no. The clerk replies, "Well, federal law says she has a right to have one." Leroy nods and wonders if he turned off the coffee pot before they left the house.

Effie is able to breathe on her own, and for the first few days everyone who loves her is optimistic. Then the test results are all finally in: Effie's brain is permanently damaged from a massive stroke, and she lapses into what Leroy calls "a deep sleep," her children refer to as a "coma" (out of Leroy's earshot) and the neurologist labels "a vegetative state." As days go by, hope fades along with viable options and most everyone's energy. The doctor finally states the obvious and confirms that Effie will not regain consciousness and she's quickly losing weight. Leroy takes the doctor's advice that the compassionate thing to do is to put Effie on a feeding tube.

At the end of the second week, Leroy feels as if he's making a dreadful decision about the next move for Effie, not that he really has a choice. The hospital will discharge Effie soon, and Leroy has to find a nursing home—a "long term care facility," the social worker quickly corrects him—even though he and Effie each said they would never go to a nursing home, and each promised never to send the other one there, either. Of his few options for affordable and decent care, Leroy chooses a facility close enough to home that he can visit Effie daily. The people there agree to admit her, estimating that with the cost of care, Leroy and Effie's net worth will last three or four more years.

The doctor making rounds at the nursing home meets Leroy and Effie for the first time when he stops by her room on the second day. He looks at Effie, at her chart and at Leroy. Then he says, "You'll need to decide if you want to withhold feeding. It would be more merciful. I mean, if you think that's what she would want." He walks out.

Leroy has been married to Effie for 67 years—known her for over 70—and at that moment he has absolutely no idea what she would want.

He goes home and spends hours sitting in his recliner, looking over at Effie's favorite chair, holding her picture and listening to the ticking of the clock the children gave them back on their 50th wedding anniversary. Leroy's not sure he wants to live in the house alone, the home they built and shared for so many years. He still supervises the boy who mows the lawn, and he cooks well enough to keep from starving, but Effie pays the bills, keeps the grocery list, tracks the certificates of deposit. Neither one of them ever expected to live alone in this house—or anywhere else. Not that any of that really matters, though, because when their daughter helps Leroy with the nursing home application, she tells him it looks like he'll need to sell the house within six months to pay for Effie's care.

Their son Junior stops by the next day. He and Leroy are having a cup of coffee at the kitchen table when Leroy breaks down and sobs, "I guess our plan didn't work."

"What plan was that, Dad?" Junior gently asks.

Leroy answers without hesitation, "We planned to die together in our sleep."

Leroy and Effie's plan definitely needed some work, and, truth be told, they knew that. From time to time, though, if some well-meaning third party brought up the subject of death or being left behind, one of them could always be trusted to laugh and say, "Don't worry about us—we've got a plan!" and the topic was dropped. So their approach to the inevitable did serve to avoid an unpleasant discussion of an unwelcome subject. But, as it turns out, wishful thinking is not a plan.

"Self-determination": the ability to act with free will. It's something most people enjoy every day and don't really think about. There's not much reason to—until it's diminishing or gone. Perhaps you've experienced an illness or injury that left you temporarily dependent on someone else for your simplest needs. Due to your condition (somewhere on the scale between being uncomfortable and being unconscious), you had to rely on the clear thinking of others because self-managing your care was out of the question. Or maybe you've been witness to a seriously ill or dying family member who was completely dependent on the good judgment and compassion of health care professionals and loved ones. Did you wonder if it's even possible to have a plan to maintain self-determination once the capacity to self-manage care is lost? Well, it is possible, because the term "self-determination" means being able to make truly informed decisions about your own care or, if necessary, having those decisions carried out by someone who knows you and knows what you would choose if you could.

If that sounds like a tall order, it may be, but once you're familiar with medical and legal options for critical and end-of-life care, you can approach the advance health care planning process armed with the knowledge and self-determination (read: power and autonomy) you need, whether you're the patient or an advocate for someone else. Then you can formulate your plan, put it on the shelf and get back to the business of living.

This chapter covers America's unique demographics and their impact on health care choices—today and tomorrow. Because, like it or not, we're all in this together.

Where the heck did all these people come from?

Sally, born in 1951, is the middle child of five. Her dad and mom marry right after World War II. They build a house for $11,000 in the new development on the edge of town, using his GI Bill, and proceed to raise their own vegetables and several kids. The house has two bedrooms (with room for expansion in the half story), one bathroom and a one car detached garage. Sally and her two younger brothers attend kindergarten in the brand new elementary school a few blocks from their home. By the time Sally gets to high school, there's a brand new one of those too.

When Sally graduates from college in 1973 with a liberal arts degree, a house like the one her parents built in 1950 has a market value of $26,000. Sally doesn't really notice because the employment market is so tight, she's lucky to get a job paying $525 a month, and no way can she afford to buy a house. In fact, she's a renter until she marries and officially becomes a DINK (Double Income, No Kids) in 1977.

And so it goes for almost 79 million Baby Boomers.

Sound strangely familiar? It's not your imagination. If you're old enough to recall the middle of the last century, close your eyes. Remember that curiously large number of spinning hula hoops? Twenty-five million were sold in one four-month period in 1958.[1] Notice all those houses popping up? Between 1950 and 1980, the number of homes nearly doubled,[2] while the median cost more than doubled.[3] And guess what explains the otherwise puzzling popularity of that quintessential couple, Barbie and Ken?

In 1946, the U.S. population was 141,388,566. By the end of the post-war Baby Boom eighteen years later, the population had increased 36 percent to 191,888,791.[4] Baby Boomers have been a demographic tsunami in the United States for almost seventy years, driving top news stories, water cooler talk and the consumer economy. There are 76.4 million Boomers today,[5] Americans born between 1946 and 1964, now aged 51 to 69. The 28 million parents of the Boomers (The Silent Generation and The Greatest Generation) are 70 and older.[6]

These two demographic cohorts account for well over 100 million Americans, and no one should be surprised ten years from now when the sixty-year-olds are seventy and the seventy-year-olds are eighty—and so on and so on. Together they will forever change how aging and the end of life is viewed in the United States.

The dying trajectory

In health care, the progression toward life's end is known as the "dying trajectory," the pattern of declining health that ends when you die. Sudden death has a vertical trajectory, a short—and usually unexpected—path from being alive to being dead. In the year 1900, a person with a terminal prognosis had the same dying trajectory now attributed to a sudden, unexpected death, about three days. Modern day terminal illnesses tend to have a protracted dying trajectory. In other words, the dying process continues over a number of months, or even years, and is characterized by a slow, gradual descent to the end of life, sometimes interspersed with short periods of stability or even improvement.

How does growing older impact your dying trajectory? In 2013, 2,596,993 people died in the United States (a number that grows each year). Up to age 44, the leading cause of death in the United States is accidents. From ages 45 to 64 the rankings shift: cancer takes first place, followed by heart disease and then accidents. For people ages 65 to 84, the top three leading causes of death are cancer, heart disease and chronic lower respiratory diseases, such as Chronic Obstructive Pulmonary Disease (COPD) and asthma. (This is a recent change; until 2011, strokes were the third leading cause of death.) It's not too surprising that when you reach age 85 and older, Alzheimer's disease slips into third place, right behind cancer and heart disease.[7] There you have it. Once you get past your accident-prone mid-forties and fifties, you are most likely to have a disease or condition that results in a longer, rather than shorter, dying trajectory.

In the United States, those aged 65 years and older number 43,145,000 and are projected to exceed 72,774,000 by 2030. By then, the 85 and older population will have grown from today's 5,887,000 to 8,946,000.[8] There's no question about it: the United States population is maturing dramatically. Currently, twenty-two percent of all United States' residents are Baby Boomers[9] and those same rebellious youth who coined the phrase "Never trust anyone over thirty!" are celebrating sixty-fifth birthdays at the rate of 10,000 per day—and will continue to do so for the next 15 years.[10]

For many of them, a parent's death is the first conscious recognition of mortality. The obit page becomes mandatory reading and class reunions grow smaller as Boomers witness the disability and dying of their peers as well. Meanwhile, the Boomers' parents are experiencing dying and death second-hand for the umpteenth time. Except for the 27 percent of American adults who claim to have given little or no thought to the medical care they want at life's end,[11] members of these two demographic groups find themselves thinking about aging and death—their own and their loved ones'—more than ever before. For both Baby Boomers and their parents, a harsh reality is becoming increasingly evident: all journeys to the end of life are not equal, and there are circumstances that look like they just might be much worse than death.

Of those 2,596,993 deaths in 2013, 73 percent were aged 65 and older and 86 percent were aged 55 and older.[12] These large and growing demographic cohorts— you can see where this is going—also happen to be the ones with the most protracted and complicated ends of life, health care wise. That's a challenging combination.

Competition for housing, health care and services

The potential crisis for Social Security, Medicare and Medicaid has been widely publicized. But there are other shortfalls that are bound to occur in the coming decades, such as the inevitable scarcity of age-appropriate housing and health care related resources. The mass exodus of retiring employees is already causing shortages of nurses, doctors, therapists and legal/tax/financial advisors. Unfortunately, the scarcity of consumer goods, services and mature workers—the ones with the skills that come only with experience—will coincide with an unprecedented number of people seeking those age-related products and services.

Baby Boomers are about to share a grim reality on a grand scale, one that the Boomers' parents are already experiencing. Both demographic groups live in a society ill-prepared to provide for the end-of-life needs of its aging residents—logistically, socially and spiritually speaking. Here are more enlightening facts on aging and end of life in America:

- The Boomers' parents make 19.4 million visits to emergency rooms each year.[13]
- Twenty-five percent of the annual Medicare budget is spent in its recipients' last year of life.[14]
- Consistently when surveyed, 80 percent of Americans would prefer to die at home,[15] but only 25 percent manage to do so, although that number has increased in the past 20 years.[16]
- About 29 percent of older Americans live alone. Only 4.1 percent of those 65 and older live in nursing homes—sorry, long-term care facilities.[17]
- Sixty-seven percent of adult Americans are concerned about the costs, potential pain, discomfort and loss of dignity associated with life's end.
- Only 28 percent of American adults have written advance directives; there's 65 percent participation for those over 68 years of age. (Good news: these numbers have been creeping up over the past few years.)[18]
- Forty-seven percent of Americans have had a relative or friend with a terminal disease or in a coma in the past five years. Half of them had to face the issue of whether or not to withhold life prolonging measures from their incapacitated loved ones.[19]

Decisions about everything from housing to end-of-life care are and will continue to be influenced, to some extent, by a person's available support systems. In 1970, with a national population of 205,052,174, the average household size was 3.14 persons, and 17 percent of homes had four or more children.[20] Since then, the U.S. population has increased to 311,375,655, but family size has shrunk to 2.64 persons, and only 2.1 percent of those households have more than three children.[21]

The birth rate (the number of live births per 1,000) was 24.1 in 1950. Today that rate is 12.6.[22] In 1950, only 9.3 percent of U.S. residents lived alone; now 29 percent of homes are one-person households.[23] What do all these numbers mean? That a person with a prolonged and debilitating illness is less likely than in the past to have children and housemates to assume the role of caregiver. Timing's everything, isn't it?

The real significance of these statistics is that the issues surrounding aging and end of life that were far off on the horizon a few years ago have slowly crept into our collective consciousness. They will be in our faces in the coming decades as the Baby Boomers confront the process of aging and dying. And it's not just the raw numbers that are extraordinary. Actually, in updating data for this *2015 Edition*, it is quite jarring to see that there are 25 million fewer parents of Boomers and 1.6 million fewer Boomers than in 2006. What is equally remarkable is that the Baby Boomers will account for such a large (dare I say overwhelming) proportion of the population; an unprecedented number of aging persons coping with the medical, moral and legal implications of the modern dying process, while competing for a dwindling supply of age-appropriate services.

In the past, the failures of our free market and the government to provide the supply for every Boomer demand in a timely manner have often resulted in shortages followed by higher prices, and the Boomers learned to adapt. For example, Boomers had to pay more for their first homes, which deferred some dreams, but for decades the Boomers' mere presence led to some of the greatest economic growth ever known in the United States, which was good for everyone. Tradeoffs. However, when it comes to age-specific services and goods that Boomers will want and need, that's quite a different dilemma. Adequate health care and end-of-life care are not widgets or hula hoops. This time, it's not realistic to ask Boomers to kindly take a seat while the nation gears up production to manufacture more medical professionals, caregivers and suitable health care and housing facilities. Aging and dying have neither conscience nor patience.

How far into this health care crisis will we get before someone notices those 76,000,000 people knocking at the door—again?

Each person's willingness to take responsibility for his or her own health care and end-of-life decision making becomes increasingly crucial, on both the individual and societal levels, as our culture's values and priorities are put to the test. And we know this for certain: the attitudes and responses of the Boomers' parents, the Baby Boomers and the Echo Boomers (the Baby Boomers' children) will be shaped as virtual probabilities morph into stark realities throughout the coming years and decades.

Four Simple Steps (not necessarily in this order)
to having effective health care advance directives

Answering these two questions is key to planning an end of life that respects and maintains your right to self-determination—even if you are incapacitated:

- What are my options for critical care and end-of-life care?
- What can I do to ensure that my choices are respected if I am incapacitated?

The underlying rational for advance directives is the assumption that there may be a time in the future when you are no longer able to manage your health care. Your incapacity may be temporary, like being under anesthetic during surgery, or it may be long-term and irreversible, like having Alzheimer's disease. Preparing and communicating health care directives in advance ensures that your physician and those speaking on your behalf know what kind of medical care you want and how you wish to be treated in a medical crisis and at the end of your life.

You are going to learn about the two types of written advance directives, the Durable Power of Attorney for Health Care and the Living Will. You will see that the process of creating effective advance directives to give others the information and authority they need to honor your wishes is made up of four simple steps (not necessarily in this order):

- **Education** – Understanding the legal implications of and medical options for critical and end-of-life care is key to managing your health care and creating meaningful and effective advance directives.
- **Delegation** – If you ever need a proxy decision maker, you'll want the one best suited to advocate for you and your care instructions. It's important to first understand the proxy's rights and responsibilities and the criteria for choosing someone to act as your proxy.
- **Communication** – Once you've considered your options and chosen your proxy, learn how to have that crucial conversation with your proxy, an alternate proxy and other loved ones, giving them the information they may someday need to act on your behalf. Shared decision making means knowing how to obtain and process medical information and treatment options, which requires effective communication with health care professionals.
- **Documentation** – Meaningful written advance directives preserve your wishes for care and give your proxy the necessary authority to make decisions in keeping with your preferences. You'll learn how to choose the legal forms best suited for you and how to share and safeguard that paperwork.

It's one thing to learn about the legal and medical elements of health care decision making, and, without a doubt, that is fundamental to the task of creating effective advance directives. But what truly makes it all come together for you and your loved ones won't be found in the pages of this book. It is the experiences, beliefs, spirituality, cultural background, relationships, health and attitudes that you bring to this process. It's the bits and pieces that make up the distinctive <u>you</u> that are vital to crafting advance directives that will communicate to your physician and loved ones what to do on your behalf, if and when you can't speak for yourself. It really is.

You'll maintain self-determination by taking responsibility for your health care plan and giving yourself and your loved ones the gift of a lifetime: knowing your wishes and taking the steps necessary to ensure that they are honored.

Why do you need to know this?

Only about 28 percent of all American adults have executed written advance directives. One might assume that those who haven't done so are suffering from a bad case of either denial or dread. Not so. The most common reasons cited by those without advance directives are a lack of information and because it was never discussed with them.[24] What you're doing right now—reading this book—is proof that you're determined to not be one of them. If a lack of information is the only thing standing between you and effective advance directives, here you go.

No really, why do I need to know this, you ask.

Because "advance health care planning" means becoming familiar with treatment and care options and making considered choices ahead of time, which makes for truly informed consent in the future. This is a good time (the first of several) to reiterate that if you are still competent in a medical crisis or at life's end, you can continue to manage your own care. You are the "self" in "self-determination" as long as you maintain the capacity to give informed consent for medical treatment. Statistically, the majority of Americans will remain compos mentis to the very end and will still be calling the shots. Once you have the needed information on health care and end-of-life options, you'll be truly prepared to make those decisions. That's the number one reason you need to know this.

Secondly, if it turns out someone has to step in and make decisions on your behalf, then having this knowledge and communicating it to your physician, proxy and loved ones means they'll understand what you understand. They'll have the benefit of your thoughtful consideration ahead of time, which may eliminate a lot of confusion in the midst of a crisis. With effective communication and written advance directives, your advocates will be fully informed and fully authorized.

There's a third reason to get familiar with this terminology and the options that modern health care has to offer. If the situation ever arises, you'll be a more competent decision maker for someone else, because you'll already understand the lingo and—more important—your role and responsibilities as proxy.

Those are the three reasons you need to know this: if you remain competent and in charge of your own care, if you're incapacitated and your life is in the hands of a fully informed proxy or if you're called upon to be a knowledgeable advocate for another person. That about covers it.

No matter what prompted you to take this first step toward managing your health care and end-of-life care—for your own sake or for the sake of your loved ones—you're off to a great start.

How this book is organized

- You now have an understanding of how end of life in this country may change in the coming years and why it's in your best interest to do what's necessary to maintain self-determination in managing your health care.
- **Chapter Two** focuses on the history of the written advance directive that contains instructions for critical and end-of-life care, the Living Will.
- **Chapter Three** is about the written advance directive known as a Durable Power of Attorney for Health Care, which is the appointment of a proxy decision maker.
- **Chapter Four** continues the discussion of the Durable Power of Attorney for Health Care—expanding on the topics of incapacity, the powers of the proxy, guardianship and criteria for choosing a proxy.
- **Chapter Five** provides a comprehensive look at definitions and the practical application of legal and medical concepts relating to critical and end-of-life care. First and foremost, it's important to understand when advance directives concerning life prolonging measures become effective by recognizing whether a triggering event has occurred.
- **Chapter Six** is devoted to hospice and palliative care. Forty-three percent of all deaths in America now occur while under hospice care.
- **Chapter Seven** covers communication, which is key to successful advance health care planning, how to have the crucial conversation with your proxy and loved ones, and how to practice a shared decision-making process with health care professionals.
- **Chapter Eight** addresses the "what ifs" of advance directives.
- **Chapter Nine** explains what to look for when choosing the best advance directive forms and how to take care of those documents once they're executed. It pulls everything together from previous chapters, with a **Review and to do** list.
- **Chapter Ten** is an introduction to the subject of Ethical Wills. Not a legal document, an Ethical Will is a record of what you stand for and how you want to be remembered. It can be an important foundation for effective advance directives, as well as value-inspired estate and charitable giving plans.
- **Chapter Eleven** is a fact-based rant. There's no other way to put it.
- Each chapter ends with a **Chapter Review**.

- To find the state-specific sources you will need, look to the references in **For further information** at the back of the book. For the explorer in you, check out the **Endnotes**.
- For readers who are not really hip to using the Worldwide Interweb, sorry, but that's where the information about states' advance directive laws and suggested forms can most easily be found. If you're short on computer skills, get long on chocolate chip cookies, and find a hungry teenager to access web sites and print information for you.
- The pronoun "he" is used for ease and no other meaning should be inferred.

It's important that you begin—and finish—the task at hand. You've taken the admirable first step of opening this practical guide, and it is meant to make the process of creating effective health care advance directives as user-friendly and easy-to-follow as possible. There's a bonus in this *2015 Edition*. As this is *The practical guide to Health Care Advance Directives*—not the *Now you're on your own guide to Health Care Advance Directives*—there are practical hints sprinkled throughout the book. They look like this:

Lightbulb moment! They appear anytime I think you can benefit from extra information on how to approach an issue, or I have a suggestion on what might make your journey go a bit more smoothly or I came across a story or just something fun to share with you.

Here's the first one:

Lightbulb moment! Go to your state's data center (try "population projections for [state]" in any Internet search engine), and discover the future aging demographics for your state. Then visit your state's agency on aging (or department of elder affairs, etc.), and find out if your state is preparing for what may come.

The right time to make an end-of-life plan

The right time to make a plan for managing your critical and end-of-life care, in case you are incapacitated in the future, is while you still can. The time is now.

Chapter Two
The Living Will:
Instructions for your care and feeding

The time to repair the roof is when the sun is shining.
John Kennedy

Delores considers herself a responsible person, someone who exercises daily and eats a balanced diet, not someone drifting through life, flapping in the wind with a "que sera sera" attitude. She reads somewhere that she should have advance directives, but she isn't quite sure how to go about doing that. Then she talks to a friend who knows about such things, and she tells Delores that first she has to talk about her wishes with the one person she trusts most in the world. For Delores, that would be her husband Bob. Delores does what her friend recommends. She shares her wishes for care with Bob and makes him do the same. In the meantime, she asks other people what advance directive form they're using, discovers that most aren't using one at all and keeps looking.

Delores and Bob arrive at the outpatient surgery center bright and early, as instructed. The admissions clerk Judi has Delores take a seat across from her in the cubicle and begins to review the paperwork that always seems to accompany a visit for a medical procedure. In a drone-like voice, Judi asks Delores, "Do you have advance directives for health care?"

Delores says, "Well, yes, but not written ones—not yet—but I'm working on that."

It's almost as if Judi doesn't even hear her answer, Delores thinks, because Judi goes on to say, "Well you have the legal right to have advance directives. Please sign right here, acknowledging receipt of a copy of our policy." She slides the form across the desk to Delores.

Delores looks at the "Disclosure re: Federal Patient Self-Determination Act" and finds the place where it asks if she has formulated (formulated?) an advance directive. It lists a Living Will and a Durable Power of Attorney for Health Care. Delores just needs to check off "YES" or "NO." She looks up at Judi.

"Is it okay if I write something in at this place here?" Delores points to the left of the "YES" and "NO."

Judi's head jerks up and her eyes suddenly focus. "What do you mean?"

"I don't have any written documents, those ones named there, but I have my husband with me, and he's my proxy and he knows exactly what I want if a decision has to be made. I've given him my verbal directives."

Judi is flummoxed. This is a new one.

Oh great, what am I supposed to do now, she wonders. No sense asking anyone around here. When she started this job, Judi questioned the purpose of the form, and it turns out nobody understands what it means. What the heck, this lady seems to know what she's doing. Judi shrugs. "Sure, I guess so."

So Delores writes "My husband Bob Smith is my proxy and he knows my wishes. Ask him." She signs the form and smiles as she slides it back to Judi. "Thank you, Judi."

"Oh, sure, you're welcome." Judi makes a mental note to mention this later in the break room. They have a daily "Bet you've never heard this one before" pool. This one is a winner, for sure.

It's scary out there, out in the world of legal and medical mumbo jumbo. This chapter is the first of the four simple steps (not necessarily in this order) to having effective health care advance directives: **education**.

Why here and now?

Starting to understand what's behind the pervasive—one might even say annoying—parade of commercials about reverse mortgages, affordable burial insurance and frequent trips to the bathroom? The numbers game. Consider that in 1900, there were *three* million U.S. residents aged 65 and older. Today, that number is over *forty*-three million.[25] In 1900, life expectancy was 47 years.[26] Currently it's 76.4 years for men and 81.2 years for women.[27] A person with a terminal disease was given about three days to put his affairs in order in 1900,[28] and nowadays that prognosis is more likely to be measured in months or even years. As noted in Chapter One, the causes of death most likely to result in a prolonged process of dying—a protracted dying trajectory—creep to the top of the list as Americans age. Couple that with a growing menu of life extending medical treatments and you have a whole lot of people demanding a whole lot of complex health care services. There's a real advantage to being among those prepared to deal with it all.

Advance directives

Right now you're still able to make decisions concerning your medical care, but you think it might be best to have a fallback position if that's not the case down the road. You've worked long and hard to build a meaningful relationship with your doctor. You may even have shared what medical procedures you want—and don't want—if you're incapacitated at the end of your life. That's admirable, but what are the chances you'll remain under your personal physician's care in a medical crisis? A trip to the emergency room or any procedure requiring a specialist may exclude your personal physician, and if you're hospitalized, there's an increasingly good chance you'll be seen by a "hospitalist," a doctor who makes rounds on behalf of clinicians, or an "intensivist," a physician who specializes in intensive care. You'll be meeting them for the first time—and not under the best of circumstances. Okay, assume for the moment that your own doctor is the one overseeing your critical care. Is it realistic or fair to expect him to accurately recall those heart-to-heart conversations you've been having over the years? And let's be real, it's doubtful if either one of you have predicted the exact medical condition in which you'll find yourself.

There is really only one way to make sure your critical care and end-of-life wishes are known and respected if you can't communicate and that is by having advance directives. "Advance" implies a time prior to the occurrence of a specified medical condition or emergency and prior to the patient's incapacity. A "directive" is a document or order meant to guide or direct actions. The function of advance directives is to act as a record of what treatment you want in certain medical situations; they are your instructions and preferences for care, prepared in advance of the circumstances so that, if necessary, someone else can step in and follow your orders.

Comprehensive advance health care planning incorporates the appointment of a proxy decision maker, the medical and comfort care you want, how you want to be treated by those around you and any message you want to leave with your loved ones.

Verbal vs. written advance directives

The terms "Living Will" and "Durable Power of Attorney for Health Care"—or similar variations under state law—are the ones that people recognize and are most familiar with, but it's no longer accurate to suppose that all advance directives are legal documents. You'll see that the label "advance directives" also includes verbal statements of what you want to happen—and not happen—if you are unable to communicate in the future. Not that verbal advance directives are the legal equivalent of their written cousins, because they are not (more about that in Chapters Four, Eight and Nine), but what you say to your loved ones about your wishes for care is no less important than the instructions and preferences recorded in your documentation.

The term "advance directive" or "directive" in this book refers to verbal <u>and</u> written instructions. In reference to the legal document known as an advance directive, you will see the terms "written advance directive," "a Durable Power of Attorney for Health Care," "a Living Will," "an advance directive form" or "a combination advance directive."

The Durable Power of Attorney for Health Care

Any medical condition or procedure has the potential of rendering the patient unable to manage his own care. Let's say you're having your tonsils taken out. During surgery, the doctor discovers a small nodule in your throat and recommends its removal as well. If you didn't give consent for that before surgery began and you're now unconscious, can the surgeon proceed without authorization? No, so how does he obtain your informed consent without waking you?

You (the "principal") previously executed a Durable Power of Attorney for Health Care and named someone (the "proxy," "health care proxy," "surrogate," "health care agent" or "substitute decision maker") to make health care decisions for you in the event you cannot give informed consent. Your spouse is your proxy, so the doctor consults with him in the waiting room, and he agrees that the growth should be removed now. After surgery, you wake up in the post-operative suite, and your husband/proxy is no longer in charge because you've regained the capacity to self-manage your medical care.

The Durable Power of Attorney for Health Care is the document that contains the appointment of a health care proxy in the event you become incapacitated. In the case of a combination advance directive, the portion of the document in which a proxy is appointed is the same as a Durable Power of Attorney for Health Care.

The Living Will

You're back in surgery for a minor issue, but this time an unexpected tragedy occurs: you have a massive stroke while under anesthetic. A few days later, the doctor delivers the really bad news to your husband that you have suffered irreversible brain damage and are now in a persistent vegetative state. Although you continue to breathe on your own, your nutrition and hydration must be provided through a stomach tube and an intravenous line. Since you are only 52, there is no reason to believe you will not live to your full life expectancy in this condition. The doctor turns to your husband, who is grief-stricken and sleep-deprived, and asks the big question: "What do you want me to do?"

Luckily for your husband, you not only named him as your proxy in your Durable Power of Attorney for Health Care, you took another important step and had a Living Will drawn up. A Living Will contains instructions for the use of life prolonging measures in the event of a "triggering event," a terminal or irreversibly incapacitating condition specified by the "declarant" (the person executing the Living Will; in this case, you). Its function is to guide both the medical professionals' care and your health care proxy's advocacy. In the case of a combination advance directive, the portion of the document in which life prolonging measures are addressed is the same as a Living Will.

Even better, you and your husband didn't just sign Durable Powers of Attorney for Health Care and Living Wills, you also discussed some medical scenarios that might happen and shared with each other your preferences in each situation. Your physician and your husband can read that your Living Will specifies no artificial nutrition or hydration is to be administered to you except on a short-term basis.

Otherwise, you want to be allowed to have a natural death without tubal feeding if the condition is irreversible, which yours certainly appears to be.

Is it easier for your husband to authorize either the withholding or withdrawal of a feeding tube, knowing you will die soon after, because that's what your Living Will says to do? Maybe, but probably not. Your husband can, however, authorize that procedure without wondering whether you would agree because it's your express wishes he is enforcing.

You can now see the distinct purpose of each written advance directive: the Durable Power of Attorney for Health Care contains the appointment of a health care proxy, granting decision-making authority in all medical situations. The Living Will, addressed to the physician and other caregivers, contains instructions for the use of life prolonging measures in the event a triggering event has occurred. Ideally, advance directives delegate decision-making authority and give health care professionals and the proxy the information they need to act as the patient would, if the patient could.

Judicial history behind the Living Will

The idea of a Living Will, a document specifying a person's preferences for life prolonging procedures, was first introduced in the United States in 1949 by the Euthanasia Society of America. It gained no recognition at the time, probably due to the stigma of the organization's stated objective, which was to promote the cause of what was then known as "mercy killing" and is now known as euthanasia.[29] In 1967, attorney Luis Kutner reintroduced the idea of a Living Will, and the Euthanasia Educational Fund drafted and distributed a model version. Thanks to a 1973 newspaper column by the late Abigail Van Buren ("Dear Abby") promoting the concept, publicity and demand for the document grew. By 1978, three million copies of a Living Will form had been distributed.[30]

At about the same time, Americans were first introduced to the "right to die" movement—the right to refuse life prolonging measures (life support)—through the names and faces of two young women. Let's see how the nation ended up bearing witness to the final chapters of their lives.

Karen Ann Quinlan

For reasons still unknown, 21-year-old Karen Ann Quinlan quit breathing and fell into an irreversible coma on April 15, 1975. Her condition deteriorated and within weeks she was declared to be in a "chronic persistent vegetative state" without any hope of recovery. Three months later, Karen Ann's family asked for the removal of the ventilator, that she "be returned to her 'natural state'." The hospital first agreed and then refused to allow the withdrawal of the mechanical ventilator.

The Quinlans took their cause to the New Jersey Superior Court where they lost. Not surprising for a 21-year-old forty years ago—or even today—Karen Ann Quinlan did not have a Living Will specifying whether to withhold life prolonging medical treatment in such a situation. The court held that prior verbal statements made by Karen Ann to the effect that she never wanted to be kept alive by extraordinary means did not rise to the level of a "living will" premised on informed consent relating to her current circumstances. The Quinlans appealed and prevailed in the landmark case, *In the Matter of Karen Quinlan*. In March of 1976, the New Jersey Supreme Court granted the Quinlans' request to reinstate Karen Ann's father as guardian and ruled that if her personal physicians concluded there was no reasonable possibility of Karen Ann's recovery from her present comatose condition and a medical ethics committee concurred, then the ventilator could be removed.

After the agreement of all parties specified by the court, Karen Ann was weaned from the ventilator although her father chose to leave her feeding tube in place. Contrary to the opinion of numerous medical experts who had testified that she would die within a year on the ventilator, and that her death was imminent once it was removed, Karen Ann survived for another nine years. Karen Ann Quinlan passed away on June 11, 1985.[31]

Until the *Quinlan* case was decided, "brain death" was the standard used to measure whether the removal of artificial respiration was legally justified. Karen Ann was not brain dead; she was in a chronic persistent vegetative state (today, it would probably be labeled a permanent vegetative state) for which there was and is no known therapy for improvement or cure. The brain in a permanent vegetative state still controls body temperature, breathing, blood pressure, heart rate and, to some limited extent, chewing, swallowing, and apparent sleep and wake cycles. So pioneering was the New Jersey Supreme Court's ruling, it included an unequivocal statement that the removal of the ventilator would not constitute criminal homicide by any of the parties involved.[32]

Quinlan addressed the issue of withdrawing a ventilator. The next landmark court decision involved a different life prolonging measure: artificial nutrition and hydration.

Nancy Beth Cruzan

On January 11, 1983, Nancy Beth Cruzan, 25 years old, was thrown from her car in an accident that left her lying face down with severe facial and internal injuries. When emergency personnel found her, Nancy was in cardiopulmonary arrest; she was not breathing and her heart had stopped beating. She was resuscitated by the paramedics but never regained consciousness on any level. Much like Karen Ann Quinlan, Nancy Beth Cruzan was in a permanent vegetative state, but unlike Karen Ann, Nancy did not need a ventilator.

Believing at the time that it would ease feeding and further Nancy's recovery, within weeks of the accident her parents and husband consented to having a tube inserted for nutrition and hydration. Four years later the family asked for its removal, a request that was denied by the state-owned hospital caring for Nancy. The litigation of *Cruzan v. Director, Missouri Department of Health* began in 1987. The Missouri trial court agreed that Nancy's family could ask for removal of the feeding tube, relying on statements Nancy had made to her housemate that "she would not wish to continue her life if sick or injured unless she could live at least halfway normally . . ."

The State Department of Health appealed that decision to the Missouri Supreme Court, which did not agree with the trial court and disallowed the removal of the tube, stating, ". . . no person can assume that choice for an incompetent in the absence of the formalities required under Missouri's Living Will statutes or the clear and convincing, inherently reliable evidence absent here."[33] You see, unlike New Jersey's statute, in order to allow the removal of artificial nutrition and hydration, Missouri law required clear and convincing evidence of the patient's intent. The Missouri Supreme Court disagreed with the trial court's holding that Nancy's previous statements were reliable proof of her wish to withdraw the feeding tube.

The Cruzan family appealed this state court decision to the U.S. Supreme Court. In *Cruzan v. Director, Missouri Department of Health, et al.* (1990), the country's highest court agreed that the right of informed consent means a person must first grant permission for any medical treatment (which includes artificial nutrition and hydration) and may also demand the withdrawal of a treatment. Acknowledging that this right continues even if the person is incapacitated, the U.S. Supreme Court weighed the patient's rights against the state's interest in protecting human life and agreed with the Missouri Supreme Court that it is constitutional for Missouri's living will statute to require "clear and convincing" evidence of the patient's specific intent to have artificial nutrition and hydration withheld or withdrawn.

U.S. Supreme Court Chief Justice Rehnquist pointed out that requiring clear and convincing evidence of the patient's wishes avoids an erroneous decision, which maintains the status quo and allows for the "discovery of new evidence regarding the patient's intent," among other possible changes in circumstances.[34] As William Colby, attorney for the Cruzan family, observed, "After all we'd been through, the thousands of pages written, could the case really have come down to just eight words?"

William Colby said that because in 1988, just after the Missouri Supreme Court disallowed removal of the feeding tube, a woman had come forward, a 1978 co-worker of Nancy. At the time, William Colby filed her comments away for possible use in the future. Soon after Chief Justice Rehnquist's prophetic words in the U.S. Supreme Court decision, that co-worker and another provided credible testimony in a hearing before a Missouri probate judge. They testified as to statements made by Nancy in reference to a severely disabled child they had all worked with 12 years earlier. At the time, Nancy had stated she would never want to be tube-fed. In probate court, Nancy's physician spoke in favor of discontinuing the artificial nutrition and hydration, and the Cruzans were allowed to withdraw the feeding tube on December 13, 1990, almost eight years after Nancy's accident. Nancy Beth Cruzan died on December 26, 1990.[35]

The *Quinlan* and *Cruzan* cases are not significant because of the off-chance that you or a loved one will end up in a permanent vegetative state. Thankfully, the odds of that are minuscule. Rather, it is the courts' confirmation of each person's retained right to informed consent, even when incapacitated, and the courts' guidance for acting on behalf of another that lifts these cases to landmark status. Karen Ann's and Nancy's stories also illustrate how important it can be to preserve self-determination by making an unambiguous record of your wishes for care while still competent.

Right behind the judges came the lawmakers

Laws governing advance directives, both verbal and written, are left to each state. California passed the first statute recognizing a Living Will in 1976. Forty more states did the same within a decade, and by 1997, all fifty states and the District of Columbia had provided for advance directives of some sort in their state codes. Not to be upstaged, the U.S. Congress wanted to get in on the new movement toward preserving one's preferences for life prolonging measures.

State Living Will statutes

Not every state recognizes the concept of a Living Will, although they all provide for some method of advance health care decision making. Oh, and the states that do refer to a Living Will don't all refer to it as a Living Will. There are also "directives," "declarations," "directives for medical services," "declarations relating to the use of life sustaining treatment," "declarations as to medical or surgical treatment," "life prolonging procedures declarations" and "declarations of a desire for a natural death."

The timing of the new statutes dealing with end-of-life decision making in the 1970s and 1980s was no fluke. They followed on the heels of the Quinlan and Cruzan families' very public legal battles and understandably so. For millions of Americans, those cases raised frightening and seemingly unanswerable questions: *When is enough enough?* And—most troubling—*Could something like this happen in my family?*

Disregarding the issue of labels for the moment, are all Living Wills created equal? Not really. Some state statutes and even dictionaries take the position that a Living Will is a document that declares your intent to decline life prolonging measures if your condition is terminal or you are irreversibly unconscious. In these "default option" Living Wills, the directive to withhold life prolonging treatment is automatic, an attempt to avoid the perceived tragedies of the *Quinlan* and *Cruzan* cases. True, one person may want his Living Will to specify that under those circumstances, there are to be absolutely no life prolonging measures of any kind, no way, no how, but the next person might have a different attitude. He may want his Living Will to say, "Bring it on—I want anything and everything done up to the time Saint Peter takes my hand!" The differences are obvious.

It's interesting to observe that default option Living Wills were promulgated as a way to avoid someone from being "doomed to no more than a biologically vegetative remnant of life," as stated in the *Quinlan* decision. With all due respect for these well-meaning legislators and lexicographers, apparently they didn't notice it was the strongly-held religious beliefs of Joe Quinlan, Karen Ann's father, that led him to leave one life prolonging measure in place (the feeding tube) while he authorized the removal of another (the ventilator). That's the lesson to be learned from the litigation surrounding end of life for Karen Ann Quinlan and Nancy Beth Cruzan: written advance directives are not the place for groupthink. A Living Will is meant to express health care directives based on the individual's personal values and right to moral independence—the meaning of "autonomy." Notwithstanding the opinion of some others, this book adopts the definition of a Living Will as the declarant's preferences as to the use of life prolonging measures in the event of a triggering event—without any inference about what those preferences are.

Lightbulb moment! Locate and bookmark online sources for accessing your state's advance directive laws by first visiting the **For further information** page in the back of this book. You may even want to print any summary or overview provided by a government agency or bar association in your state. (In Chapter Eight, I'll cover how crossing state lines affects the enforceability of your advance directives.)

The Patient Self-Determination Act (PSDA)

Not long after the *Cruzan* case was decided, Congress passed the Patient Self-Determination Act of 1990 (PSDA). It applies to most health care facilities (hospitals, skilled nursing facilities, nursing facilities, home health agencies, providers of home health care and hospices). At the time of admission or the start of services for a patient, the provider is required to do the following in reference to advance directives (meaning <u>written</u> advance directives):

1) Provide information in writing about patients' rights under state law, concerning medical care and advance directives and the provider's written policies concerning those rights and any limitations.

2) Document in the patient's record whether the patient has an advance directive at the time of admission.

3) Avoid conditioning the patient's care or otherwise discriminate depending on whether the patient has an advance directive.

4) Ensure compliance with applicable state laws regarding advance directives.

5) Provide education for the facility's staff on policies regarding advance directives.

6) Provide community education regarding advance directives.[36]

Note that the PSDA requires compliance with state advance directive laws, which is not the same as requiring compliance with an individual's advance directives. State laws usually address any objection to carrying out a patient's wishes by allowing the provider to transfer the patient to another provider.

There is no requirement under the PSDA that the patient receive assistance in executing written advance directives at the time of admission. If, however, the provider does offer an advance directive form to the patient, the patient is not obligated to execute it. The patient should clearly understand and be in 100 percent agreement with any document he signs. The admissions process is neither the time nor place to address this, especially if the patient has a well-informed proxy available. But it may serve as a needed prompt to address the issue of written advance directives soon after, if appropriate to the patient's situation.

Lightbulb moment! The next time you interact with a PSDA-covered provider—as a patient or as a patient's proxy—be sure you get a copy of the provider's policy concerning patients' or clients' advance directives. Then read it to make sure there are no restrictions or limitations. An institution is permitted to have a "conscientious objection" to the application of a person's advance directives, but it also has an obligation to inform patients or clients of that policy upon admission.

Has the existence of the PSDA increased the number of American adults with written advance directives? It's true that participation has grown from 15-20 percent in 1990 to the current rate of 28 percent. However, credit for that non-seismic shift is probably due more to our aging demographics, because the older you get, the more likely you are to have written advance directives. There really isn't enough research to know for sure. There are, however, quite a few studies showing a pervasive lack of understanding about advance directives on the part of both health care professionals and the general public. So if health care agencies are complying with the staff and community education requirements of the PSDA, those provisions of the law don't seem to be working all that well.

Theresa Marie Schiavo puts the system to the test

The most recent case to draw wide public interest in end-of-life issues is that of Theresa Marie Schiavo. The forty-one-year-old had been in a permanent vegetative state for fifteen years when she came to our collective attention in 2005. Theresa had no Living Will, and her husband Michael sought to enforce what he claimed were her verbal advance directives to withdraw any life sustaining procedures (in Theresa's case, a feeding tube) if she was ever in such an irreversible medical condition. The Florida probate court held that Theresa's husband Michael had satisfied the three-prong test previously set forth by the Florida Supreme Court and ruled that Michael Schiavo should be allowed to discontinue his wife's artificial hydration and nutrition.[37]

Theresa's parents, Robert and Mary Shindler, sought to overturn the decision and have Michael removed as Theresa's guardian. What followed were years of judicial and legislative turmoil as the Florida legislature, its governor and even some in the U.S. Congress attempted to override existing Florida law and bar the removal of Theresa's feeding tube. The U.S. Supreme Court refused to hear the case no less than four times. The parents of Theresa Schiavo finally exhausted their legal remedies and were bound by the Florida Court of Appeal's holding that the case was ". . . about Theresa Schiavo's right to make her own decision, independent of her parents and independent of her husband." In applying the Florida statute,[38] it found that the trial court had correctly ruled there is clear and convincing evidence that Theresa's previous statements supported her husband's request to withdraw her feeding tube.[39] It was removed on March 18, 2005. Theresa Schiavo died on March 31, 2005.[40]

Schindler v. Schiavo demonstrates the unrealistic goal of crafting written advance directives or state laws that anticipate and provide a remedy for every potential conflicted situation. Florida law adequately addressed the absence of written advance directives, but even if Theresa had executed a Living Will specifying her wish to avoid tubal feeding and hydration, this court battle might still have been waged. Her parents fought against the withdrawal of life prolonging measures based on their assertion that a triggering event had not occurred; they argued that Theresa was not in a vegetative state and that her medical condition was neither terminal nor irreversible. They further asserted that there was a new treatment available that would allow Theresa to regain her cognitive function.[41]

The Florida law provides that the proxy's actions must be supported by any known patient preference. However, unlike the case of Nancy Beth Cruzan in Missouri, if Theresa Schiavo had not voiced her opinion on what she wanted for life prolonging measures, as her husband testified, the Florida statute would have allowed Michael Schiavo to make the decision on behalf of Theresa, keeping her best interest in mind. Florida law permitted substitute decision making for the withholding or withdrawal of artificial nutrition and hydration. Missouri did not.

The *Schiavo* litigation confirmed what previous decisions have consistently held: it's up to the states to make laws concerning the use of life prolonging measures and proxy decision making, and it's up to residents to know their state's law and govern themselves accordingly. That's just the way it is. The 51 individual statutes created since 1976 were intended to establish uniformity in applying end-of-life directives for the residents within each jurisdiction, not across state lines. In *Cruzan*, the U.S. Supreme Court addressed the constitutionality of Missouri's law, but that does not equate to a national standard for end-of-life decision making.

> **Lightbulb moment!** It's important to determine whether the advance directive law in your state has any unusual provisions concerning the withdrawal of artificial nutrition and hydration or any other life prolonging measures. If it is not clear from your reading of the law or public information sites, you may wish to visit with an attorney before you get too deeply into the planning part of this process—state provisions could impact how you think about your choices for care and your selection of a health care proxy.

The advantages of having a Living Will

You shouldn't have a Living Will just because it's the prudent thing or the responsible thing or even the caring thing to do. Do it because it's the smart thing to do. Who stands to benefit when there's a thoughtfully created Living Will? The answer is two-fold: 1) the patient who wants to maintain self-determination concerning his health care treatment, and 2) the people entrusted to do what's in the patient's best interest while honoring his wishes and values. In the midst of a health care crisis, that's the enduring value of a Living Will: knowing what the patient would choose if he were able to choose.

It's not possible to predict with certainty whether a particular person will suffer a particular medical condition, but we can estimate the probability of needing written advance directives in general. In a study reported in the New England Journal of Medicine, 42.5 percent of the 3,746 subjects (aged 60 and older) required some degree of decision making about their medical treatment in the final days of life, and when that time came, over 70 percent lacked decision-making capacity. That's when one would hope to refer to a Living Will for guidance. But only 66 percent of those who needed proxy decision making had written advance directives. (Sixty-six percent? Don't be shocked, the 28 percent statistic cited in Chapter One applies to *all* adults—the likelihood increases with age.) For the one-third of those who needed medical decisions and hadn't prepared Living Wills, someone had to step in and make choices on their behalf.[42] Whether those substitute decision makers had the benefit of any previous conversations with their patients about treatment preferences is unknown. It's nice to think they did.

Some truly positive news came from the study: of those who had a Living Will, there was strong agreement between the care they requested and the care they got, those with a written advance directive were less likely to receive all medical treatment possible, the surrogate decision makers felt that the Living Will was relevant to most choices they needed to make, and those who had appointed a health care proxy were less likely to die in a hospital.[43] Likewise, other studies have confirmed that those with written advance directives more often receive preferred care, and their surrogates have fewer communication issues near the end of the patient's life. Not surprising, there are also monetary savings with patients who have written advance directives and, ergo, receive fewer costly end-of-life medical treatments.[44] Not that this is just about the money, but it is partly about the money.

Even if you aren't in the estimated 30 percent of the older population that will need proxy decision making, there's another good reason to go through the process of education, communication, delegation and documentation. If you do end up managing your own health care at the end of your life—and it looks like most folks probably will—you'll be way ahead of the game by having thought about what quality vs. quantity of life means to you and having a solid grasp on treatment options and terminology.

Lightbulb moment! Before going any further, do you already have written advance directives? If so, find them (the originals, if possible) and keep them available for reference as you read on. If you can't find them, or aren't sure if they exist, would you have had them prepared by an attorney? If so, call to get a copy. If they either don't exist or are nowhere to be found, all the more important to keep moving along so you can get new ones executed as soon as possible.

Chapter review

- There will be a greater number of persons experiencing a protracted dying trajectory, which increases the need for public awareness and understanding of the importance of planning for end-of-life health care management.
- The only way to make sure your health care and end-of-life wishes are known and respected if you are incapacitated is by having health care advance directives.
- "Advance directive" includes *verbal* statements of what you want to happen—and not happen—if you are unable to voice your opinion later. The enforceability of those verbal statements depends on state law.
- A Durable Power of Attorney for Health Care is the document that contains the appointment of a substitute health care decision maker in case the principal is unable to give informed consent.

- A Living Will specifies wishes for care should a triggering event occur. A triggering event is a terminal or irreversibly incapacitating condition named by the declarant.

- The landmark legal cases concerning Karen Ann Quinlan and Nancy Beth Cruzan clearly established the right of a proxy or guardian to make legal decisions on behalf of an incapacitated patient, subject to any state law restrictions on the surrogate decision maker's authority.

- The federal Patient Self-Determination Act of 1990 requires that health care providers make patients aware of the right to have advance directives and prohibits discrimination by a health care provider on the basis of whether the patient has an advance directive.

- The Theresa Schiavo litigation reaffirmed that health care decision making is the province of state law.

Chapter Three
The Durable Power of Attorney for Health Care: Delegating decision-making authority

Chance favors only the prepared mind.
Louis Pasteur

In spite of having her share of heart palpitations and near misses, Edna's in pretty good health for an 81-year-old. Looking back, she's experienced a lot of life—and other people's deaths—and she knows one thing for darn sure: when her time does come, she has no intention of lingering helplessly between the two dimensions as many of her friends and family have done. With that in mind, on her 80th birthday Edna has her attorney prepare her advance directives. He uses a one-paragraph Living Will form right out of the state code which says everything Edna needs it to say: no life prolonging measures, no exceptions. As simple as simple can be.

Then he helps Edna complete and sign a Durable Power of Attorney for Health Care. Edna never married and doesn't have any children, but her nephew Rodney—her brother Clifford's boy—has always been thoughtful of his Aunt Edna, so she names him as her proxy. She knows she needs someone who will make the doctors follow her wishes, and Rodney's a bit of a bully, so Edna's pretty sure he'll do what has to be done. To be certain, she carries copies of both advance directives in the pocket of her apron, which she wears during all waking hours except when she's going to the store or church.

Four years later, on a beautiful spring morning, Edna is planting her bulbs and has a major heart attack right in the middle of the tulip bed. The ambulance driver finds the dog-eared advance directives in Edna's pocket and gives them to the emergency room nurse. Aunt Edna is so organized she even has nephew Rodney's phone number on the Durable Power of Attorney for Health Care. The nurse reaches Rodney by phone and he rushes to the hospital.

When he arrives, Aunt Edna is unconscious and having trouble breathing. The doctor asks Rodney, as Edna's health care proxy, if he wants her to have the assistance of a ventilator. Rodney responds resolutely, "I had no idea Aunt Edna named me as her proxy! She was such a fighter, I'm sure she'd want to live. Let's do whatever we can to help her do that, shall we?" In a matter of days, Edna is transferred to Sunnyvale to live in a permanent vegetative state with the aid of a ventilator and feeding tube.

Edna is among the 28 percent of adult Americans who have executed advance directives, both a Living Will and a Durable Power of Attorney for Health Care. She knew exactly what she wanted, and she thoughtfully named a strong advocate as her proxy. Oops. Looks like she missed one important step in the advance health care planning process. Because Edna never asked Rodney if he was willing to serve as her advocate, she also never communicated what he was supposed to be advocating for. Edna's Living Will ended up safely stowed in the back of her medical file, unread. Very safe and hopelessly ineffectual.

The importance of **delegation** in advance health care planning is covered in the next chapter. This chapter addresses the **documentation** that gives enforceability to that delegation. (You've probably already figured out that pretty much every chapter is about **education**.)

The Durable Power of Attorney for Health Care

"Durable Power of Attorney for Health Care" is a very long term containing important elements that merit individual attention.

"Durable": Unless a power of attorney says it's durable, it isn't, so its authority terminates once the principal becomes incapacitated. Since the whole point of a written advance directive is to transfer decision-making power upon the principal's incapacity, use of the word "durable" is essential. It means the proxy's authority takes effect once the principal is unable to make decisions.

"Power of Attorney": This document grants authority to a proxy or agent to act for another person, the principal. It can also refer to the authority being assigned. ("I'm acting under the power of attorney my brother granted to me, recorded in his power of attorney.") The appointed agent or proxy is the "attorney-in-fact," as opposed to someone who is trained in the law, an "attorney-at-law."

"Health Care": This book focuses on health care matters, although a power of attorney can be executed relative to assets or anything else. The authority given to a proxy or agent applies to health care decision making only if it says it does.

You gotta love state sovereignty. There's a plethora of different terms used throughout the United States that all mean the same as "Durable Power of Attorney for Health Care," like "medical durable power of attorney," "designation of health care surrogate" and "appointment of health care agent." Durable Power of Attorney for Health Care is the label of choice in this book. (Refer to the sources in **For further information** at the back of this book to find your state's preferred language.)

Professionals who specialize in estate planning and legal incapacity issues have their own vocabulary as well, which can sometimes be confused with advance health care planning terminology:

- General Power of Attorney: A power of attorney authorizing an agent to transact all business for the principal, as specified in the document. It does not include the power to make health care decisions unless it says it does.

- Durable Power of Attorney for Financial Matters: This grants authority for the agent to manage the principal's financial assets and property once the principal becomes incapacitated, but not the authority to manage the principal's health care. This is not an "advance directive" because, although it takes effect upon incapacity, "advance directives" refer to matters of health care only.
- Last Will and Testament: An instrument that provides for the disposition of a person's real and personal property upon death and for the custody and care of dependents.
- Trust: An entity created for the purpose of holding assets by the trustee for the sake of beneficiaries. There are many types of trusts: revocable, irrevocable, living/inter vivos, testamentary, charitable, etc.
- Ethical Will: Not a legal document at all, it is a record of a person's beliefs and values, life lessons and hopes for the future. It is created for the purpose of sharing one's ethical legacy with loved ones.

You may already have one or more of these documents, depending on your personal estate planning needs. Comprehensive written advance directives will complete your portfolio of essential legal documents. By the way, it is not advisable to create complex legal documents as an online do-it-yourself project. When it comes to estate planning documentation, it takes a real live, in-person attorney to get the job done properly.

> **Lightbulb moment!** As long as we're talking about legal forms that are <u>not</u> advance directives, I encourage you to have your legal and/or financial advisor review all of your estate, incapacity, charitable giving and end-of-life documentation, if that hasn't been done lately. Because these documents can be interdependent, plan to include that review when you visit your attorney to have your advance directive forms prepared.

The right to delegate health care decision making

Before the creation of the document known as a Durable Power of Attorney for Health Care there was common law, the U.S. Constitution and its amendments, all implying an individual's right to privacy. Every American is protected from unwanted touching, which includes medical treatment, and that includes life prolonging measures. Informed consent means voluntarily agreeing to, refusing to agree to or requesting the withdrawal of a medical procedure with a full understanding of the associated foreseeable risks, benefits, possible alternatives, uncertainties and the option of having no treatment. To protect the right to privacy and unwanted touching, each person must grant informed consent for any medical procedure, subject to specific exceptions, such as a medical emergency.

What if the patient is not competent and he can no longer manage his own care because infirmity, injury or incapacity diminishes his ability to give informed consent? Courts in cases like *Quinlan* and *Cruzan* have recognized that the only way to prevent destruction of a patient's right to privacy is to allow someone else to render a decision on what the patient would do, if able.[45] The right to have a surrogate make health care decisions on behalf of another is sometimes referred to as a "springing" power because the proxy's authority springs into existence as soon as—and only if—the principal loses decision-making capacity.

This means health care providers are bound by law to respect the authority of a legally recognized proxy decision maker. When that appointment is made in writing by the patient prior to incapacity, it is usually through a Durable Power of Attorney for Health Care or some variation thereof, now recognized throughout the United States.

The principal and the proxy

The principal executes a Durable Power of Attorney for Health Care in which he names someone to act as his proxy, the person authorized to stand in the principal's shoes and to make decisions the principal would be entitled to make, if able. In this book the terms "proxy," "agent," "surrogate" and "substitute decision maker" are used interchangeably. As for those freewheeling legislators, you'll find your state's label somewhere in this list: "attorney in fact," "health care representative," "representative," "health care attorney in fact," "medical power of attorney representative" or "health care agent."

Why is the proxy so darn important?

If you would agree to read only 26 pages of this book, it should be this chapter and the next. They're that important. Back at the beginning of the book, this question was posed: Is it possible to maintain self-determination—to continue to manage your health care—even if you lose your capacity to make informed decisions?

Well, one way would be to have a Living Will that addresses the exact end-of-life medical condition you'll have in the future, a Living Will that your health care providers have read and fully understand. Oh, and be sure to only retain health care providers who are willing to honor every instruction contained in your Living Will without prompting.

That doesn't sound very probable. What's my next option, you ask.

The proxy. The proxy is the guardian of patient autonomy. His role is to make health care professionals aware of the patient's directives or guide them with his substitute decision making if there are no directives on point. That's actually the proxy's number one job: to act as enforcer of the principal's preferences for care as expressed through his written and verbal advance directives or based on his general values. Just because you can no longer self-manage your care does not mean you lose the right or the ability to maintain self-determination. You can maintain self-determination if your trusted proxy knows you, is ready, willing and able to respect your expressed wishes and has a pretty good idea of what you would decide if you could—even in situations you didn't cover ahead of time. Those elements were all missing from Edna's plan.

The principal's decision-making capacity

The purpose of a Durable Power of Attorney for Health Care is to designate someone to be there when the patient cannot be, mentally speaking. By the terms of the document, the proxy's authority is durable, intended to commence and remain in effect as long as the principal is unable to make health care decisions for himself. By the way, when is that, exactly? What is the triggering event for decision-making authority to pass to the proxy?

Under some states' laws, the term "competency" refers to a court's legal finding that a person has decision-making capability. In common usage, however, "competency," "decision-making capacity" and "capacity" have all come to mean the mental ability to understand the nature and consequences of a situation or problem, make a decision regarding it and comprehend the effects of that choice. The customary language of a Durable Power of Attorney for Health Care is similar to "no longer able to make my own health care decisions" or "if I become incapacitated" or "when I am unable to make and communicate decisions, as certified according to state law."

It's a fact that the decision-making authority of a Durable Power of Attorney for Health Care is not limited to end-of-life situations, so it's easy to recognize a few obvious examples of a principal who lacks capacity: someone under anesthetic during a surgical procedure, in a coma caused by a traumatic brain injury or in a permanent vegetative state. Those are all clear cut. It could be argued, as it was by Theresa Schiavo's parents, that the medical condition is reversible and not permanent, but that goes to the issue of whether the proxy should consider the withdrawal of life prolonging measures, not whether the principal lacks decision-making capacity. Theresa Shiavo's incapacity triggered the springing power of a proxy, whether or not everyone agreed that her husband was the appropriate choice, or that it was a permanent condition triggering the option to remove life prolonging measures. It was Theresa's prognosis that was in dispute, not her incapacity.

Criteria for determining when the power of the proxy becomes effective are provided in each state's law, and every person is granted the presumption of capacity until the contrary is shown. If a diagnostic procedure is specified by statute or in a directive, it often says that the patient must be determined by one or more physicians to currently lack decision-making capacity. Keep in mind that the ability to communicate is not necessarily synonymous with competency; a person may be able to talk but lack the capacity to give informed consent. Incapacity can also be partial; a person can be competent to make some decisions but not others. And sometimes a medical condition or medication causes disorientation and the temporary inability to reason. The patient's physician has the duty and expertise to review the medical record, observe real-time behaviors, and to question the patient (if possible), the proxy, and family members who really know him. If necessary, a psychiatric consultation may be advisable to fully assess the patient's level of decision-making capacity.

Judging capacity or competency is art as well as science. Each patient's condition and circumstances are unique, and it is a collaborating team of health care professionals, the proxy and involved loved ones that can best design a decision-making strategy and treatment plan that fully respect the patient's autonomy and level of decision-making capacity.

The beginning and end of the proxy's power

The proxy's authority to make decisions on behalf of the principal is no more or less than expressly stated in the appointment document, and that applies to the when as well as the what. A Durable Power of Attorney for Health Care usually states that the proxy takes charge once the principal becomes unable to make health care decisions. That does not imply a permanent shift in power; if and when the principal regains decision-making capacity, the proxy's authority ends.

Revoking the appointment of a proxy

The proxy's power begins upon the principal's loss of decision-making capacity, but the principal may have the legal right to revoke (cancel) the proxy's appointment and its accompanying authority even after it has taken effect. Under what circumstances that can be done is according to state law. Some allow verbal revocation, some require it to be in writing and in some states a doctor must agree that the patient has regained competency.

Note, however, that a state's law may include a presumption that the principal always retains the capacity to revoke. In other words, even if everyone (except maybe the principal) agrees that the principal lacks absolutely all decision-making capacity, if he can communicate, he retains the statutory authority to fire the proxy. What? That may not seem to be in the best interest of the principal/patient (because clearly, it is not), but it's for others to debate the logic of such laws. They are what they are.

For the record, it is legally permissible for a principal to specify one or more persons in a Durable Power of Attorney for Health Care whom the principal does not want appointed as his decision maker in the event the named proxy and alternate proxy are unable to serve. The role of health care proxy is indeed a very important role; if there's a potential appointee who, in your opinion, would not be an appropriate advocate for you, by all means, say so—in writing. Even in the absence of any legal precedents addressing the enforceability of such a directive, if it's that important to you, include it.

> **Lightbulb moment!** If your state's law allows a proxy appointment to be revoked by a principal who lacks capacity, it may be prudent to seek the formalities of a guardianship once the principal/patient has been determined to be incapacitated. Definitely seek competent legal counsel for a potential situation such as this.

Guardianships

An alternative to having a Durable Power of Attorney for Health Care in place is to establish a guardianship. A guardianship is a court-ordered relationship that follows a hearing and a finding of incompetence. It gives the duty to care for an incompetent person (the "ward") to another person (the "guardian"), subject to court supervision. In some states "guardianship" refers to the person and/or the person's assets; in other jurisdictions, a guardian oversees the person while a "conservator" oversees the person's finances and property under a court-ordered "conservatorship." The power granted to a guardian may be plenary, meaning the ward loses all rights to manage his own affairs, or a limited guardianship can be ordered in which the ward maintains some rights, based on his level of capacity.

To establish a guardianship, a petitioner (a family member, friend or a social service agency) files a petition with the court. All parties are given formal notice of the hearing and a "guardian ad litem" (or "special guardian" or "next friend") is appointed to advocate for the respondent (the alleged incompetent person). The guardian ad litem evaluates the respondent and then reports his findings to the court. As part of the guardianship hearing, the court requires a showing of a specific cause for the respondent's lack of competence, evidence of how it affects his decision-making capacity and testimony on the potentially dangerous safety or health issues.

Going the guardianship route is not to be undertaken lightly. The ward's ability to govern his own affairs is at least partially abdicated, and that's a shift in authority not easily reversed. Costs of creating and maintaining a guardianship should be considered as well. Because the legal procedure can take weeks—or even months, depending on the court's availability and any resistance to the petition—guardianship is an impractical solution for many medical situations.

Many states have what is called a "standby guardianship" by which a person executes all necessary paperwork while still competent, naming someone as his guardian and specifying the mental or physical conditions that constitute triggering events. If that time comes in the future, filing the petition is a simple procedure, and this method of delegating decision-making authority has the advantage of recognizing a guardian who was hand-picked by the ward. (Caution: watch the terminology, because in some jurisdictions, a "standby guardianship" refers to a procedure for naming a backup or temporary guardian if the first appointed person is unavailable.)

Lightbulb moment! If you've already decided that you're going to use an attorney to assist with preparing your written advance directives—or you haven't yet decided—make a note now to ask him or her about standby guardianships in your state, and whether that is an option you should be considering for yourself or a loved one.

Protection for the "friendless"

Another consequence of our society's mobility—as well as its aging demographics—is an increase in the number of persons without a family member or friend who is available and/or willing and/or able to act as proxy or guardian. They are referred to as "friendless" or "unbefriended" persons. Depending on your state's law, the means to protect these folks from financial exploitation and abuse and to provide for decision making on their behalf is handled in one of two ways.

Public guardians. Every state now has some form of public guardianship program, based on a version of one of these models: 1) the court model, in which the guardian is an official of the court; 2) a state agency formed under the executive branch of government; 3) a social service agency administered by the state; or 4) a public guardian agency or officer established within each county, appointed under county government and supervised by the state's attorney general.[46] The public guardian may be an agency or an individual, most likely an unpaid volunteer.

Professional guardians. The industry of professional guardians has flourished to fill the need unmet by public guardian agencies and volunteers. Individuals, private non-profit agencies or for-profit entities act as guardian for a fee, paid from the ward's assets.[47] It's up to each state to establish minimum requirements of expertise, experience and integrity for professional guardians—or not. Ten states as of this writing require some type of certification for a person to serve as a professional guardian.[48]

Adequate oversight to protect wards' welfare and assets is a function of the supervising court system, supported by the regulatory authority of a state or local agency, and it is in direct proportion to sufficient funding and capable administration. Along with the nationwide shortage of guardians, there is a lack of reliable data on the incidence of elder abuse, statistics on state-by-state needs for advocacy and viable solutions for this growing predicament. A nation's greatness is measured by how it treats its weakest members, or so said Mahatma Gandhi. Time will tell.

Lightbulb moment! You're conscientious about the issue of advance health care planning. I know that because you're reading this book. If you're also a person of high integrity and compassion, maybe you should consider volunteering as a guardian for those without family or friends. At least find out how the issue is handled in your jurisdiction, and encourage your public officials to make compassionate advocacy a priority for one of the most vulnerable segments of our society.

The guardian vs. the proxy

Aunt Edna is living out her years at Sunnyvale when along comes niece Mary Jane (another of Aunt Edna's heirs). She doesn't share her aunt's high regard of cousin Rodney, so while he's on an extended safari in Africa, Mary Jane files a petition to establish a guardianship for Aunt Edna. The guardian ad litem reports to the court that there is no question about Edna's lack of capacity, and Mary Jane gets herself appointed as guardian. She immediately heads to Sunnyvale to give the staff her thoughts about Edna's care, waving her court appointment in their faces. As a matter of fact, inasmuch as Aunt Edna's once sizeable estate is being quickly depleted, Mary Jane voices that it is obviously in everyone's best interest to put an end to this ridiculous waste of financial resources, and she sets out to give Aunt Edna's dying trajectory a little nudge. She orders Edna's doctor to schedule the removal of the ventilator and feeding tube.

But wait! Nephew Rodney pays a visit to Sunnyvale as soon as he returns from Africa and discovers what cousin Mary Jane (she's been a troublemaker since she was little) is up to. And just in the nick of time.

Not so darn fast, Mary Jane. Where Edna resides, state law provides that if there's a dispute between the court-appointed guardian and the patient-appointed health care proxy, the proxy trumps the guardian. That's right, deference is given to the Power of Attorney granted to Rodney by Edna while she was still competent. In fact, folks like Edna and her niece Mary Jane are exactly who the legislators were thinking about when they made that law. Rodney tells the doctor to stand down and tells his cousin Mary Jane to take a hike.

Whether you come down on the side of Rodney or Mary Jane—and one could easily argue that neither one is serving Edna's best interests—it remains that Rodney is the one Aunt Edna chose. A little over half of the states agree that in a dispute, the health care proxy duly appointed by the patient overrules the court-appointed guardian. That seems fair. The other states either don't address it or give deference to the guardian. You know what's next: Check your own state's law.

Even if there's no showdown, it's important to recognize that any care preferences expressed by the ward while competent—verbally or in writing—should be respected by the court-appointed guardian. Not all states' laws call for this, but the courts have. (The real tragedy here: Mary Jane's plan is actually more in keeping with Aunt Edna's directives, even though Mary Jane's motive is twisted. Is Rodney ever going to ask if anyone knows whether Aunt Edna had a Living Will and what it says?)

Lightbulb moment! If it's possible and appropriate, naming the original patient-appointed proxy as the guardian avoids proxy/guardian conflicts. If there's a good reason to name someone else instead, the proxy should make the appointed guardian aware of the ward's advance directives, both verbal and written, and be prepared to step back in as decision maker, if necessary.

Advance directives for special circumstances

There are some situations that call for unique documentation to ensure that decision-making rights are properly preserved. These are circumstances when it pays to sit down with an experienced estate, elder law or family law attorney and get valuable input on how best to safeguard special interests.

Power of Attorney for already incapacitated adults

When someone is responsible for the care of another, advance planning should include the appointment of a replacement caregiver or guardian if the original person is unable to perform his duties. For instance, if you are the sole caregiver and health care proxy for your elderly mother and you become incapacitated, who's going to look out for Mom and make her health care decisions?

A Power of Attorney for the care of disabled or elderly adults can address this situation by naming a contingent or backup caretaker for the already incapacitated or infirm person. Many states' laws also provide for a standby guardianship, which allows a carefully chosen surrogate caregiver to be named ahead of time.

Power of Attorney for the medical treatment of minors

Similar to the Power of Attorney for incapacitated adults, there is a specialized form by which a parent or guardian can grant short-term authority to make emergency health care decisions for a minor child. Example labels are "Temporary Medical Power of Attorney for Child" or "Power of Attorney for Consent to Medical Care for a Minor." Parents who are unavailable for extended periods of time or want to address the possibility of a medical emergency can appoint a family member, trusted friend or even the child's professional caregiver as proxy. Many states also have standby guardianships, allowing parents to pre-plan for their own incapacity or unavailability by making arrangements ahead of time for a pre-selected guardian to step in.

With satellite phones, Skype and e-mail, unavailability is virtually a thing of the past, but there may still be occasions when a written Power of Attorney is appropriate for the care of minors. Consult legal counsel to ensure that the authority granted is appropriately limited and properly documented.

> **Lightbulb moment!** At the risk of being a buttinsky (although it may be too late for you to be concerned about that), if you have grandchildren and if the circumstances fit, do the parents a favor, and bring this issue of a medical emergency power of attorney to their attention for consideration. It's one of those things busy parents may not have even considered.

Psychiatric or mental health advance directives

The right to consent or refuse medical procedures applies to mental health treatment as well. A competent person living with a mental illness may choose to have a separate Psychiatric Advance Directive to address mental health treatment issues and/or to appoint a mental health proxy to oversee medication, the use of electroconvulsive therapy, hospitalization and the notification of loved ones. Twenty-five states have statutes that provide for mental health advance directives. This does not preclude the creation of a psychiatric advance directive document in the other states, it simply means you should first verify whether your state has a statutory procedure in place. Also, some states don't allow a health care proxy to consent to mental health treatment for a principal unless expressly authorized to do so in the written advance directive, so including that authority or having a Psychiatric Advance Directive may eliminate the need for a competency hearing and court-ordered guardianship.[49] It's another instance when expert legal counsel is vital.

A word about nonhuman family members

Currently, there are about 319 million people in the United States.[50] In their households are approximately 70 million dogs, 74 million cats, 8.3 million birds, 4.9 million horses and a goodly number of fish, rats, rabbits, turtles and ferrets. Six out of ten pet owners (read: pet roommates) consider their pets to be family members.[51] If you are lucky enough to be chosen to share your home with animals, you may already know what's coming next. People love their pets. Pets love their people. Kids of the four-legged variety cannot survive without their human companion to provide for their well-being. At a minimum, pet owners should speak to a trusted friend about caring for pets in the event the owner is unable to do so. To play it really safe, execute a Power of Attorney appointing a proxy to make care and medical decisions for Sparky if you cannot. No kidding.

Now you know why the proxy is so darn important

You now have a better understanding of the role a health care proxy plays in having health care advance directives known and respected. Without a well-chosen and properly appointed advocate, the enforcement of your Living Will instructions can be jeopardized. Just ask Aunt Edna.

Chapter review

- Every competent person has the right to informed consent, which means voluntarily agreeing to—or refusing to agree to—a medical procedure with full understanding of the associated foreseeable risks, benefits, possible alternatives, uncertainties and the option of having no treatment.

- The right to informed consent includes the right to have another person exercise that right on your behalf if you lose the capacity to do so.

- Capacity is the mental ability to understand the nature and consequences of a situation or problem, make a decision regarding it and comprehend the effects of that choice.

- The power of the health care proxy is effective once the principal lacks decision-making capacity and ends if the principal regains the ability to understand and give informed consent to medical care.

- A Durable Power of Attorney for Health Care is revocable by the principal according to applicable state law.

- A guardianship is a court-ordered relationship that follows a hearing and a finding of incompetence. The duty to care for a person lacking competency (the "ward") is granted to another person (the "guardian"), subject to court supervision.

- "Friendless" and "unbefriended" persons are those who do not have a family member or friend who is available and/or willing and/or able to act as health care proxy. That role may be filled by a public guardian or professional guardian, according to state law and the availability of resources.

- When both a patient-appointed proxy and a court-appointed guardian are in place, state law may prioritize their decision-making authority in the event of a conflict.

- Special documentation should be considered for the continuing care of an already incapacitated person, for the protection of minors, for those who may have a mental illness and even for pets. Yes, pets.

Chapter Four
The key to effective advance directives:
Your proxy is your voice

Always be nice to children—
they are the ones who will choose your rest home.
Phyllis Diller

Edgar sits at his desk. His advance directive forms lie before him, complete except for one little detail: the name of his health care proxy. Edgar's wife passed away five years ago, so that leaves their four adult children. Let's see . . .

His son, the oldest child, is a wonderful person who happens to live in England. Mark him "logistically challenged."

The second oldest is really the smartest one—not that Edgar would ever say that out loud. She has a career in the medical field, an administrator for an enormous California chain of clinics and hospitals, so she hangs around doctors and nurses all the time. She speaks the lingo and she's actually pretty well-known in her field; health care professionals and such might be more likely to listen to her.

The next one is Edgar's alpha child, the middle daughter. Always coordinates family events, a born leader, knows where all the important documents are kept (she should, she put them there). She lives four hours away in Pennsylvania, and Edgar remembers back when his wife died suddenly, Marge-in-Charge was the one who put together all the funeral plans and got the estate handled lickety-split. She's a whiz at stuff like that.

Then there's the youngest child. She's quiet but she's no pushover and she still lives here in town, just a few blocks away. She always seems to stop by for a visit just when Edgar is feeling a bit lonely. Fascinated with family history and genealogy, she spends countless hours talking to Edgar, asking him about his parents, about his life, about what his and his wife's dreams were when they were young. He'll never forget the day she looked right at him and said, "Dad, now that you're seventy-eight, do you have any regrets? I'll bet you've got one of those secret Bucket Lists, don't you?"

Edgar shares his thoughts about life and death with this one—stuff the others don't even ask about and maybe don't even want to hear. Who knows. Edgar takes a deep breath and considers his options.

First elimination: the son in England. It's just not practical. Even though he's the oldest. The eldest daughter has an advantage with that medical background, but she's also least likely to get away from work quickly in an emergency. True, she's always been willing and able to come in a hurry when needed. And she is the smartest. Just ask her. "Marge" is the natural choice, of course. She's the one who steps up to bat in every crisis. There's no question of her being intimidated by a doctor or anyone else—she doesn't take any guff.

There's not a one of them who isn't willing to do it, he knows that. But what he really wants is someone who knows him as a person—not just as "Dad." If only his wife was still here. But she isn't.

It's definitely the youngest, he decides. She won't be afraid to speak up—she has too much respect for her dad to let him down. Anyway, she's the one who can tell doctors what Edgar would choose. It sounds a little weird to say this about his own kids, but she's the only one who really knows him. Now comes the tough part: someone has to tell Marge . . .

As you saw in Chapter Three, the health care proxy is the key to making sure that patient preferences for care are respected. Having a proxy is important, all right—but equally important is having the right proxy.

Even with the most prudent and comprehensive preparation, there can definitely be situations you and your proxy didn't discuss or anticipate. If that happens, your care depends on 1) your proxy's understanding of and advocacy for your general character and beliefs and 2) your proxy's own value system and good judgment. That means you should know as much about your proxy's moral compass and character as your proxy knows about yours. This chapter shows how to choose the best proxy, once you've fully identified what you expect the proxy to do. This is where the importance of **delegation** becomes obvious.

Lightbulb moment! Were you able to find your advance directive forms? If you did, refer to them now, and see who you appointed as your proxy and alternate proxy. Still good with your choices? Whether or not you already have written advance directives, as you work your way through this chapter, think about your potential field of contenders and who the best choices might be. Who has the ability, willingness and availability to be the advocate you will need and want in a health care crisis?

The role of the proxy

Before choosing the person best suited for the job, it's important for the principal to fully understand the proxy's role. And before the proxy agrees to serve, it's important for him to understand what he's signing up for.

The proxy's job description

The role of the proxy is described in the principal's Durable Power of Attorney for Health Care, a standard form which has changed very little in the past few decades. Standing in the principal's shoes, the proxy has the same right to informed consent the principal would have if fully capacitated, so the proxy should be authorized to do and be willing to do any or all of the following:

- Be familiar with the principal's specific instructions for health care or end-of-life care in any written advance directive (a Living Will-type document), as well as any preferences and wishes verbally expressed by the principal.

- **(The proxy's most important role)** Act as communicator and enforcer of the principal's wishes as expressed in his written and verbal advance directives. It's very unlikely the attending physician will ask to see the principal's Living Will—instead, he'll rely on the proxy to share the principal's instructions. That's the way it is and that's okay.

- Know the principal's values, his beliefs on what quality of life means and his definitions of independence, self-sufficiency and being well.

- Meet with health care providers to receive medical information about the principal's condition and prognosis, to get explanations of medical procedures and to seek specialists and second opinions as warranted; consider the benefits, risks of and alternatives for treatment options, and consult with the principal's health care team to formulate a treatment plan.

- Consent to, refuse to consent to or withdraw consent for medical procedures or care, which may include life prolonging treatment or medical procedures intended for curative or palliative (comfort) purposes.

- If necessary, be willing to take legal action to enforce the principal's wishes.

- Arrange for the principal's admission to or transfer from a health care, rehabilitation or residential care facility.

- Hire or dismiss health care, social service and aid workers to provide for the principal's competent and compassionate medical and personal care.

- Review the principal's medical records, and consent to the appropriate disclosure of those records to others, such as an insurer, care facility or health care professional.

- Take steps to ensure that the principal receives all insurance, Medicare and Medicaid benefits to which he is entitled.

What the proxy's responsibilities do not include

Even though the appointed proxy is often the principal's day in, day out caregiver as well, a proxy is not responsible for providing hands-on physical care of the patient by reason of being named proxy. The proxy's duties may, however, include arranging for, consenting to and overseeing that care. The proxy's role also does not include the duty—or the authority—to access or manage the principal's financial matters. That responsibility must be granted in a separate Durable Power of Attorney for Financial Matters or through a court-ordered guardianship over assets (or a "conservatorship" in some jurisdictions). Finally, the health care proxy may be asked to sign documents in a medical or care facility assuming financial responsibility for the principal's care. Whether to accept that personal liability is the proxy's decision, but acting as the health care proxy does not, in and of itself, make the proxy financially liable for the care of the principal.

 Lightbulb moment! It's a good policy in <u>all</u> circumstances to read anything you are asked to sign, <u>before</u> you sign it. If you don't understand the terms of a document, ask for clarification. And "Don't worry about it—everybody signs this" does not constitute clarification.

The beginning and end of the proxy's power

To repeat what was said in Chapter Three, the proxy assumes health care decision-making authority once the principal becomes unable to give fully informed consent to medical treatments. That shift in power may or may not be permanent, because if and when the principal regains decision-making capacity, the proxy's authority ends. To be realistic, however, the proxy should be prepared to serve indefinitely.

The proxy's role after the principal's death

By definition, the proxy's authority to make health care decisions ends once the principal dies. However, the proxy's duties may extend beyond the principal's end of life concerning two issues: disposition of the principal's remains, including authorization for an autopsy, and organ donation (more on that in Chapter Five).

The proxy's continuing role may come from instructions left by the principal or by statutory authority. Each state's law dictates whether the deceased can name someone to carry out his wishes concerning an autopsy and disposition, and whether those instructions must be honored. It's probably not surprising that the states are all over the place on this subject. Here's a sampling: your disposition instructions are respected as long as they're attached to the Durable Power of Attorney for Health Care; your disposition instructions are respected as long as they are in writing, executed in the same manner as real estate deeds; anyone can be authorized to carry out your wishes; only next of kin can be authorized to carry out your wishes; disposition instructions are honored only if you pay for them ahead of time through a funeral director; and—this one's just the best—you definitely have the right to leave disposition instructions, and your kin definitely have the right to ignore them.[52] Yipes.

If the principal intends the proxy's duties to extend past the principal's death, those specific duties should be clearly stated in the written advance directives. First and foremost, refer to your state's law on this. It may require the use of a designated form for disposition instructions, restrictions on who can be appointed as agent and even rules about where the form should be kept.

> **Lightbulb moment!** Store any detailed instructions for the disposition of your remains and any funeral, memorial or going-out-party plans where they can easily be found—<u>not</u> with your Last Will and Testament in the safety deposit box. Make others aware of your instructions verbally and in writing as required by state law, and make sure others know where any separate written instructions or plans can be found, preferably in an envelope clearly marked "IF I'M ABOUT TO DIE—OPEN IMMEDIATELY!"

Guidance for proxy decision making

There is more detail about the physician-patient and physician-proxy shared decision-making process in Chapter Seven, but, in general, when it comes to making health care decisions on behalf of the principal, a proxy should be guided by the following standards—in this order of priority—depending on a patient's unique circumstances:

- Refer to previous clear-cut written or verbal statements by the patient, if available.

- Use substituted judgment to determine what the patient would do under the circumstances, based on specific or general evidence of the patient's values, attitudes about life in general and views on how his life is meant to be lived.

- Do what is in the best interest of the patient when there is no trustworthy evidence of what the patient would want.

- Withhold a treatment if it would be inhumane to continue the treatment.

- Err on the side of preserving life (in the case of whether to remove a life prolonging measure) if no other position can be supported.[53]

It may seem like common sense to start with the most explicit evidence of the principal's wishes and work your way down the list, as the situation dictates, but this also happens to be the guidance provided by the courts. It's affirming and refreshing to observe their respect for the patient's value system as well as relying on any specific directives that may be recorded in a formal legal document.

Statutory limitations on the proxy's authority

Regardless of the language of the written advance directive, the proxy's authority may be subject to restrictions contained in state law. Over half of the states require express consent given by the principal—written in some cases, verbal in others—to allow the proxy to authorize certain procedures to be performed or withheld. The legal position in those states is that such actions are so closely tied to the patient's autonomy that they should not be allowed unless there is no doubt about the patient's intent. These state laws are similar to Missouri's "clear and convincing" standard to remove a feeding tube, the subject of the *Cruzan* case. Among health care procedures that require the principal's express permission are:

- Withholding or withdrawal of artificial nutrition or hydration (tubal feeding).
- Mental health treatment or institutionalization.
- Psychosurgery, electroconvulsive therapy or the use of psychotropic drugs.
- Sterilization or abortion.

This is another one of those times when it's important to 1) be familiar with your state's laws on advance directives and 2) as needed, include specific instructions in your written advance directives addressing restricted procedures. Verbal advance directives—just telling your proxy what you want him to do on your behalf—may not be adequate or enforceable in some circumstances.

> **Lightbulb moment!** A friend tells me her father is in hospice care in a skilled nursing facility where he has just taken a fall and broken his hip, and his physician is recommending surgery to avoid potential pain. He can't be positive, but the surgery may extend her father's life to some degree.
>
> Her father's advance directives specify comfort care only and he is to be given no life prolonging medical procedures. My friend's not sure whether to ignore her father's advance directives and authorize the surgical procedure.
>
> It would not be ignoring his directives to consent to a surgery being done for palliative purposes. Without her willingness to put a contextual reading on his directives, her father could suffer needlessly. She is considering his values and care goals and applying his care preferences to the real-life situation at hand. She is doing her job as his proxy/advocate.

Choosing the person to act as your proxy

Before discussing the characteristics you want in a proxy, let's first cover any legal restrictions on who can—and cannot—act in that capacity.

State law restrictions on proxy appointments

State laws typically require that a proxy be of a minimum age, 18 or 19 years, to ensure contractual capacity. To avoid a conflict or the appearance of a conflict, in most states certain persons or classes of persons are not allowed to act as proxy because of their relationship to the principal/patient. For instance, the principal's attending physician and any employee or owner of a care facility where the principal lives are common exclusions, although they are allowed to serve if also a relative of the principal. There can be statutory restrictions on the number of principals for whom one person can act as proxy (think: professional guardians).

Lightbulb moment! Many state laws provide that the written appointment of an ex-spouse as proxy must be executed <u>post</u>-divorce in order to be valid. The "He/she can't possibly have meant for him/her to have that kind of authority!" statutory provision makes sense.

Considerations in choosing a proxy

Since your life may literally be in your proxy's hands, <u>trust</u> is key when choosing the person best suited to act on your behalf. Understandably, there's a lot of emphasis on having a proxy who truly knows you and will stand up for you, but as essential is your familiarity with and confidence in your proxy's good judgment and how he views life. If you don't have anyone in your life that you trust to this extent, no choice may be better than a bad choice. Going proxy-free is not the same as having no written advance directives. Do take the all-important step of completing a comprehensive Living Will with detailed care instructions addressed to your attending physician. Although without a trusted proxy you bear the risk of having your directives ignored, giving verbal instructions to your physician coupled with a detailed Living Will are two big steps toward minimizing that risk.

Advocacy. It bears repeating: the one character trait required of every proxy is the ability and willingness to act as the patient's advocate. That does not necessarily mean the person with the biggest mouth, largest girth or most threatening manner. What it does mean is the one who truly knows what the principal would want, is willing to stand up to medical professionals, to ask the hard questions and to sometimes make the hard calls. Practically speaking, in this day and age, acting as the patient's advocate also means being physically present to make sure the patient is treated with competence and dignity anytime he is entangled in the health care system. Anymore, you have to be pretty darn sick to be allowed to remain in a hospital. It is a sad but true fact that our hospitals' and care facilities' well-intentioned and compassionate labor force is generally overworked and understaffed. With that in mind, the proxy should be prepared to safeguard the welfare of the patient at all times. Gettin' old ain't for sissies and neither is the modern health care system.

Availability. In a 2013 study, when dialysis patients were asked to name a proxy, for almost a third, the person named was <u>not</u> the same as the emergency contact.[54] That doesn't make much sense when you think about it. Sounds like a recipe for confusion or inaction when medical personnel expect decision making from the person who just rushed in the door, only to discover he has no authority. Review your wallet card (okay, get yourself a wallet card once you get to Chapter Nine) and make sure names and contact information are up-to-date and logical. Although it is possible for a proxy to make decisions via phone, Skype or email, immediate and direct communication with health care providers is a significant part of the proxy's duties. And can a proxy really make informed decisions without observing the patient in person over time? Bottom line: choose someone who is on hand or can get to your bedside quickly in a medical crisis. Keep in mind, the dying trajectory is more often a gradual than a steep decline, so a proxy may need to stick around and be available for an extended period of time.

Multiple proxies. It is generally not advisable to name "co-agents" and place proxy duties and power simultaneously in the hands of more than one person. In life-and-death matters, ruling by committee is a bad idea and asking for a showing of hands will lead to either consensus or discord, but more important, it may result in either a decision that disregards the patient's wishes or a stalemate. It is not practical or necessary to nominate all concerned persons as decision makers.

Alternate proxies. Naming one or more alternate proxies is quite a different matter from naming co-agents. There should always be a named successor in case your first choice is unable or unwilling to serve. The proxy-spouse is a perfect example; you know, the person most likely to be in the company of the principal—and therefore also incapacitated—if there's an accident. And remember that legal documentation can become quickly outdated if a proxy experiences his own life-changing event. A backup proxy is a good idea.

Family member as proxy. Naming your closest relative—spouse, adult child or sibling—may seem like the natural thing to do, but it may or may not be the best idea. If relatives are dealing with their own capacity issues, aren't available or are simply not the best choice for whatever reason, look outside the family circle. Close friends, domestic partners or even your attorney can be considered.

Unrelated persons as proxy. "Family" has a multitude of meanings and being related legally or by blood is not a prerequisite for being someone's proxy. The last section of this chapter addresses what happens if you don't name a proxy and state law designates a "default surrogate decision maker" or "proxy-by-statute." In that event, familial relationships definitely matter, but when it comes to appointing a proxy in a duly executed written advance directive, relation by blood or law is not relevant. Name the person best suited, related or not, and fully document that choice in a written advance directive.

> **Lightbulb moment!** I am not aware of any prohibition against someone's personal attorney serving as his health care proxy. For those without family or friends capable of taking on the responsibility, it may be that trusted legal counsel is the most suitable choice, as well as being the person who best knows the principal and is most familiar with the content of the principal's advance directives.

The crucial conversation: "Will you be my proxy?"

Ever heard the expression "Better to beg forgiveness than seek permission"? Well, it doesn't apply here. Only by explaining what is expected of the proxy, asking him to serve and having him accept can a truly effective principal-proxy relationship be established. Don't assume that just because someone is named as a proxy means he is obligated to or will want to accept the job when he discovers—in the midst of a medical crisis—that he's been appointed. If he does agree to serve, it may be with absolutely no idea of what he's expected to do. Why? Because the opportunity to clarify duties and expectations was back when the principal asked whether he was willing to be the proxy, and the principal never did that.

The importance of carefully considering the persons to serve as your advocates and having heart-to-heart conversations before appointing your proxy and alternate proxy can't be overstated. It's the fair thing to do. It's the smart thing to do.

Lightbulb moment! While we're on the subject of choosing a proxy, have you agreed to be a proxy for anyone else? Can't remember? Hmm. Ask the persons most likely to have appointed you. Then, as you learn and think about choosing proxies of your own, also consider your duties as someone else's decision maker. Is it perhaps time to visit with that person—or persons—for clarification on their expectations of you? And, for heaven's sake, get a copy of their advance directives!

Conversation starters

How do you take the first step down a path that may ultimately end with one person pulling the plug on the other? Could be awkward, you're thinking. But you'll set the tone for this conversation, so the more convinced you sound about the advantages of having effective advance directives, the more likely your choices for proxy and alternate proxy will be convinced of the same. Following here are some situations that provide opportunities to start this dialogue. But please don't misunderstand, if the occasion doesn't present itself soon after you are ready to have this important discussion, don't wait. Get the conversation started. In most cases, proxy candidates aren't surprised to be asked—they'd have been disappointed if someone else had been chosen.

- If you see a television show or movie that deals with aging or end-of-life issues, watch it together, and share your thoughts afterwards (and, thanks to the Internet, that can be anytime!).
- Reflect on the experience of a family member or close friend when decision making became an issue, whether it was a source of conflict or an example of advocacy. Either one can be a chance to talk about what went wrong or right.
- Taking an extended vacation or business trip can prompt you to get your affairs in order, and creating written advance directives can be part of that process of organization.

- A public seminar or presentation on advance directives is an opportunity to invite your potential proxies to attend with you; then have coffee and a conversation afterwards.

- When there is a planned surgery or medical procedure in your near future, knowing you will be asked about advance directives when you're admitted to the health care facility is a good excuse to discuss those issues ahead of time.

- Milestone birthdays or holiday gatherings can sometimes trigger thoughts of the passage of time and what essence of life means to you. Share your thoughts and invite your proxy choices to do the same.

- As soon as an adult child officially becomes an adult (18 or 19 years of age) and qualifies to serve as your proxy, it's an opportune time to discuss what that could mean if you have a medical crisis.

- If you are becoming an empty nester, retiring or having your first grandchild, use that important life event to address the shifting roles and responsibilities of family members.

- How about leaving this book lying casually on the coffee table—maybe it will be the conversation opener you're hoping for. Keep in mind what studies have shown: most people have failed to talk about and prepare written advance directives not because they don't want to face reality but because they don't have the knowledge they need to get started—and they don't know anyone who does. Very soon your loved ones will know someone who has the knowledge they need to get started—you.

 **Lightbulb moment!** Now, don't laugh. There's a web site called *"let's have DINNER and talk about DEATH."* Its purpose is to encourage folks to gather their friends and family to, well, talk about death. It has lots of resources and interesting stories from people who have tried this. It may not be for you, but, then again, it might be. Think Pizza and Proxies or Deep Fried Chicken and Directives. *www.deathoverdinner.org*

Any one of the opportunities listed above is an occasion to discover what your proxy and alternate proxy think about end-of-life issues in general, which will give you a chance to share your thoughts in more specific terms and then go for the close.

Taking "no" for an answer

Don't be crushed if the answer to your question "Will you be my proxy?" is "Thanks, but no, thanks." It happens. Some people are just not comfortable with this level of responsibility. Confusion over potential duties can contribute to that anxiety, so make sure you clearly explain the role of the proxy and in what circumstances your health care proxy might be called upon to act as the advocate for your directives. If the person is still reticent, ask if he can tell you why. If he can't or won't verbalize his concerns, or you can't satisfactorily address his fears, smile and move on to your next prospect. It's better to know now.

The "crucial" part of the crucial conversation

Once your proxy knows what his duties are and is willing to accept the responsibility, it's time to talk about your directives, the specifics of how you want to be treated in a critical care or end-of-life situation. This is when you do everything you can to make the role of proxy a blessing and a privilege—not a burden—for your proxy and alternate proxy. Show respect for them by communicating your instructions, both verbally and in writing and fully informing them of what you would choose if you still had the capacity to decide, rather than expecting them to rely on their own preferences or best guesses when the time comes.

Along with your proxy and alternate proxy, it's important to include other family members in this conversation, those who might be present in the event of a medical crisis. It not only allows you to explain your choice of proxies (if an explanation is warranted and appropriate), but it also allows others to bear witness to your instructions. That greatly increases the chances for informal consensus and proxy support if and when decision making is necessary. As for the specifics of the discussion, that very important aspect of **communication** is covered in Chapter Seven.

Let's say someone doesn't appoint a proxy—what then?

There's little doubt about your good intentions to execute advance directives, and you're clearly way ahead of the pack. However, there's at least a fifty-fifty chance that any other American adult won't do the same. There's also the possibility that someone may state his care instructions in a Living Will but not appoint a proxy. In either case, even if a person declines the right to appoint a substitute decision maker, he doesn't lose the right to informed consent. But there has to be a uniform method to decide who acts as proxy if the need arises. Recognizing this potential issue, all states have some form of law providing for a "default surrogate decision maker" or a "proxy-by-statute."

You might be familiar with the term "intestacy." That's when someone dies without a Last Will and Testament. In that event, the state makes assumptions about who should inherit the unclaimed assets, since the deceased didn't speak for himself. These statutes cover the prospect of a surviving spouse but no children, a surviving spouse with children, surviving children but no spouse—you get the picture. The law might say that in the case of an unmarried person with children, the children inherit everything, or if there's a surviving spouse and children, the spouse gets it all, etc.

The right to appoint a health care proxy in a written advance directive is analogous to the right to have a Last Will and Testament. Exercise your right or take your chances. Every state addresses the lack of a patient-appointed proxy by specifying a pecking order of those who can step in and become the recognized default surrogate decision maker or proxy-by-statute. Statutory lists are similar to this one (in order of priority):

- A court-appointed guardian, if there is one.
- The patient's spouse.
- The patient's adult child (ruling by majority vote if there is more than one).
- The patient's parent.
- The patient's adult siblings (ruling by majority vote if there is more than one).

Some state laws recognize a person named verbally by the patient, a "close friend," an adult grandchild or even a domestic partner. In his turn, each person on the list has the option to be recognized as the proxy-by-statute or refuse to serve.

The intent of these laws is not to designate the person you would have named if you had named someone, because the lawmakers can't possibly know who that is. The statutory approach is premised on odds and availability. They are best guesses of what is suitable for most people most of the time, not an attempt to predict what is ideal in your unique situation. If you haven't spoken to your siblings for 20 years and wouldn't care to put them in charge of your lawn care, let alone your end of life, that's a shame if you didn't make other arrangements and they're willing to do it. You have the right to record your choice with written advance directives, if you want to. For those who don't, no complaining.

Lightbulb moment! Speaking of Last Wills and Testaments, if you don't have one or the one you have was done when your grandchildren's parents were toddlers themselves, please have one drawn up. There are lots of good reasons to do that. Just one is that whether your opinion of who should inherit your worldly possessions agrees with your state lawmakers' opinion will no longer be an issue.

Thirty-seven states and the District of Columbia recognize same-sex marriage, and 12 states recognize civil unions and domestic partnerships.[55] In the 37 states with same-sex marriage, legally married partners qualify as spouses for purposes of proxy-by-statute laws. However, in order for an <u>un</u>married domestic partner to be a proxy-by-statute, a state's law must include that category of default persons, and that is true in only ten states. Unless, of course, you want to argue that the person to whom you have committed your life is also a "close friend," which will work in 25 states.[56] But, since, as the patient, you won't be in a position to argue anything, never mind.

Seriously, why even go down that rabbit hole? If your preferred choice of proxy decision maker is not recognized under your state's proxy-by-statute law—and that has to be very near the top of the list to do you any good—please execute a Durable

Power of Attorney for Health Care. And this applies to a sister-in-law who is just like a sister but, in law, isn't. Just do the paperwork and you won't have to worry.

Back to our intestacy analogy. Guess who gets all your goodies if you have no Will and there are no statutory heirs? Your state's treasury. It's similar in the case of health care decision making. For a friendless person, if there is no one on the list who exists or is willing or able to act as proxy-by-statute, a social service agency can step in and seek court protection through a public guardianship. Practically speaking, it is more likely that health care professionals will simply proceed in what they consider to be the patient's best interest. That may be due to time constraints and, frankly, a lack of concerned parties to pursue the expensive and time-consuming judicial route.

Consider who is likely to be around if you need some surrogate decision making. If you're not comfortable with the options provided by your state's law and how it might all go down, address the situation <u>now</u> with the written appointment of a proxy and alternate proxy of your choosing.

Lightbulb moment! In most states, the default surrogate decision maker hierarchy calls for "majority rule" by multiple adult children or adult siblings. Do yourself and your children or siblings a favor, and don't set them up for that. It can be a lose/lose for everyone and a formula for unresolved conflicts that can linger for a very long time. Like forever.

Chapter review

- A proxy stands in the principal's shoes and has the same right to informed consent the principal would have if not incapacitated.
- The proxy takes charge once the principal becomes unable to make health care decisions; if the principal regains decision-making capacity, the proxy's power ends.
- The role of the proxy does not include hands-on care of the patient, control of the patient's assets or financial responsibility for the patient's care.
- Duties of the proxy may extend past the end of the patient's life to include authorization for organ donation, an autopsy or disposition of the body.
- The proxy's decision making on behalf of the patient should rely on specific instructions from the principal as well as familiarity with the principal's general values and belief system.
- State law may limit the proxy's ability to consent to some procedures unless there is specific written or verbal evidence of the patient's intent.
- In choosing a proxy, consider the issues of advocacy, availability, alternate proxies and whether to name family members or unrelated persons.

- State law may disqualify some people from serving as proxy, usually the principal's attending physician and anyone associated with the principal's care facility.

- Everyday situations can provide a good starting point for your conversation with your proxy and alternate proxy candidates. But don't wait for them to occur—put this on your ASAP list.

- If no health care proxy has been appointed in a written advance directive, states' laws provide a list of potential proxies to be recognized as the patient's default surrogate decision maker or proxy-by-statute.

Chapter Five
So little time, so much to choose from

What, then, is to be done?
To make the best of what is in our power,
and take the rest as it occurs.
Epictetus

Maxine was diagnosed with Alzheimer's eight years ago and it's not as if anyone thinks she's going to recover from it. Quite the contrary. Everyone understands—and Maxine actually leads the charge on this—that once the disease has taken its toll and her heart stops, then that's it, party over, adios amigos. In fact, right after the diagnosis, while there is no question about whether she still knows what she's doing, Maxine takes her daughter Wendy along to her attorney's office.

"I want one of those DNR things. I don't want CPR or anything like that," Maxine says to the attorney in a very unambiguous manner.

The attorney smiles and says he feels exactly the same as Maxine and he knows just what to do. "You got it! I say, just pull the plug!" He prepares a Living Will for Maxine, specifying that she doesn't want any life prolonging measures if she has a terminal or irreversible condition. He keeps a copy and gives copies to Maxine and Wendy. So there.

The day Maxine doesn't wake from her nap, Wendy naturally calls 911, and by the time the ambulance arrives, Maxine's heart has stopped. Of course, Wendy is inconsolable that her mother is gone, but she isn't really surprised; it has been a very long goodbye. Her thoughts are abruptly interrupted by the emergency worker's question, "Does your mother have a Do Not Resuscitate order?"

"Oh, yes, she made sure her attorney handled that. I'll go get it," and Wendy heads in the direction of her mother's desk. But Maxine's Living Will isn't where it's supposed to be, and by the time Wendy returns to the living room, they've already started performing CPR. She tries to tell them that her mother doesn't want that, but they say they don't have a choice, because if her mother doesn't have a OOH-DNR or a POLST, they have to try to resuscitate her. That's the law.

Wendy thinks, What in the world are they talking about?

Who would have ever thought the resuscitation attempt on Maxine would be successful? She survives to go to the emergency room, but she never wakes up and she never comes home. Wendy stays at the hospital 24/7 for three days, visiting her mother in intensive care for ten minutes at the top of each hour and watching as her mother's life slips away. Maxine dies on the fourth day.

Wendy can't help being furious with herself. She keeps thinking she should have had a copy of her mother's Living Will with her at all times, so she could make sure her mother's wishes for no CPR were honored. Over and over she says to herself, "This wasn't what was supposed to happen."

As she is sorting through her mother's possessions a few weeks later, Wendy finds Maxine's Living Will. It's at the bottom of the kitchen towel drawer. What in the world is it doing there?

Where to begin? Maxine was caught in a perfect storm. Her attorney, as it turns out, did not know just what to do. He didn't give her competent legal advice, and because of that, Maxine's directives weren't properly preserved. Not to mention poor Wendy not getting the guidance she deserved from her mother's attorney or her mother's doctor, who never even brought up the subject of Maxine's options as the end of her life approached. It doesn't appear that anybody knew what they were doing.

Your advance directives should be a reflection of your belief system, your values, your sense of self and your idea of what it means to be alive and well. However, unless they're communicated in unambiguous, enforceable terms, they're not going to be of much value to you—or anyone else. Ideally, advance directives are prepared from the perspective of the declarant, but they'll have to be implemented from the perspective of the physician and proxy, and an instruction manual shouldn't have missing pages. A little later in this chapter, you'll see exactly how Maxine's wishes ended up being ignored.

Before you set out to record your preferences for care, doesn't it make sense for you to first understand the realistic options you may have—and that your proxy may have—in a medical crisis or at life's end? This part of your **education** will clarify the meaning of those choices and help you consider what to include in your advance directives.

Triggering events

Anytime you are incapacitated and a medical decision needs to be made on your behalf, your physician and proxy should refer to your advance directives for guidance. Whether the use or withholding of life prolonging measures ought to be considered at that moment depends on whether a "triggering event" has occurred. Triggering events are the medical conditions identified in a Living Will-type directive—as well as in many state statutes—for which the declarant wants specific life prolonging measures to be either administered, withheld or withdrawn.

How important are the exact words used to describe a triggering event? They can literally be a matter of life and death. The legal battle surrounding Theresa Schiavo focused on whether her condition constituted one of the triggering events under Florida law, a persistent vegetative state. If it did, her husband would be allowed to consider the removal of her feeding tube. Her parents asserted that Theresa was neither in a persistent nor permanent vegetative state and that her condition was reversible. In essence, they argued that a triggering event had not yet occurred. Ultimately, the court agreed with Michael Schiavo's medical experts who asserted that it had.

Uncertainty or outright disagreement over whether it's appropriate to be discussing life prolonging measures is certainly not unique to Theresa Schiavo's situation. In fact, knowing when the use of life sustaining measures should be considered is the 800-pound gorilla in the advance health care planning arena. As you learn about treatment options in this chapter, please remember that the proxy's first duty in a medical crisis may be to determine whether a triggering event has occurred. If it has, it's time to examine the patient's instructions addressing the use or withholding of life prolonging measures. If it hasn't, the proxy's responsibility is to advocate for full treatment for the principal, weighing burdens and benefits as appropriate for his existing condition and treatment plan.

Until recently, the triggering events specified in written advance directives were similar to these: "a terminal condition that will cause death in a relatively short time or an irreversible state of unconsciousness from which I will not recover." Terminal or irreversibly unconscious. What do these key terms really mean, and are Living Wills still doing everything people expect them to do?

Terminal condition

A "terminal" medical condition is incurable and will, at some point in the future, cause the person's death. For purposes of hospice benefits under Medicare and most private insurance companies, terminal is a life expectancy of six months or less. Relative to whether a terminal condition qualifies as the triggering event in a Living Will, it is presumed to be a prognosis of a more immediate or imminent nature, although it is not a quantifiable time period. In reality, one person may want to consider the issue of life prolonging measures because he has only months to live. Another patient may be near death from an acute condition like a sudden stroke, and without intervention, the terminal nature of his condition can be measured in hours. Although there is no bright-line period of life expectancy that defines it, practically speaking, a terminal condition in a Living Will is one which cannot be cured or reversed and that is reasonably expected to cause the patient's death within a relatively short time.

Irreversible state of unconsciousness

By 1976, the public had a vague understanding of what a coma is and it was learning what "brain death" means, but Karen Ann Quinlan's "chronic persistent vegetative state" really threw everyone for a loop. Just to be clear, here are some definitions:

- A coma is a state of deep unconsciousness from which the patient cannot be roused and there is no wakefulness or awareness. A patient may or may not wake up and recover from a coma.

- Brain death is the permanent absence of all brain activity, including brainstem reflexes, as indicated by fixed pupils and no pain response. Brain death is unquestionably irreversible, and the brain dead patient cannot breathe without the aid of a mechanical ventilator. Although it is a concept that is admittedly difficult to understand, the brain dead patient is medically dead.

- A vegetative state, which can be partially or totally reversible, is a condition of severe brain damage that has progressed from a coma to a state of wakefulness without awareness. Some limited brain function continues, and the vegetative patient has sleep-wake cycles, his eyes are often open and he may be able to breathe on his own. The "persistent" vegetative state that does not improve within months may be declared "permanent," which means it is irreversible. One source put it succinctly: "Persistent vegetative state is a diagnosis; permanent vegetative state is a prognosis."

Coma, brain death and a vegetative state each may qualify as the triggering event of permanent irreversible unconsciousness described in a Living Will or state statute, depending on the patient's exact prognosis.[57] For purposes of evaluation, there are specific tests and explicit criteria to verify the patient's medical condition; most state laws specify that two physicians must agree on such a diagnosis or prognosis.

The evolution of triggering events

An effective Living Will reflects the declarant's preferences on when and whether to administer life prolonging measures once a triggering event occurs. It's up to the declarant to ensure that the Living Will form he uses adequately defines the potential triggering events he intends to include.

Enter dementia. It encompasses several diseases and symptoms, but they all result in diminished memory and thinking skills. Alzheimer's disease, which accounts for 60 to 80 percent of dementia cases, progresses over years from the early stages of memory lapse to late-stage Alzheimer's in which the person loses the ability to respond to his environment, cannot control movements and has impaired swallowing. Its numbers are projected to increase by 40 percent in the next ten years,[58] and it is already the sixth leading cause of all deaths in the United States.[59] The second most common type of dementia is "vascular dementia," which results from a stroke, which is the fourth leading cause of death in those 65 and older.[60]

At some stage of dementia's progression, the patient's condition may be terminal, or he may be in an irreversible state of unconsciousness; either one would qualify as a triggering event in a typical Living Will. If, however, in the opinion of the declarant, being terminal or being irreversibly unconscious is not soon enough to address the use of life prolonging measures for a dementia-type condition, then he may want to ask, "When and how do I want life prolonging measures to be used or withheld if I am unable to speak, cannot feed myself or have no awareness of my surroundings?" There are now Living Will forms that include triggering events such as "an advanced progressive illness not likely to improve that leaves me unable to communicate, swallow, or care for myself" or "if I will not recover the ability to recognize my loved ones and surroundings." These are dementia triggers. And a declarant's directives for the use or withholding of life prolonging measures and care instructions need to be just as unambiguous and clear as the description of triggering events.

In February of 2014, the Supreme Court of British Columbia addressed this issue for Canadians. Margaret Bentley, now in the final stage of Alzheimer's disease, had stated in two separate directives that she wanted "no nourishment or liquids" but that she would accept "basic care" "if at such a time the situation should arise that there is no reasonable expectation of my recovery from extreme physical or mental disability." Mrs. Bentley has not spoken since 2010, does not appear to recognize anyone and her family argues that Margaret would not want to continue to have assisted oral feeding (spoon feeding). The court disagreed, noting that Margaret takes nourishment when prompted by placing a spoon or glass on her lower lip; it concluded that spoon feeding is not "health care" but instead a form of personal care or basic care, which should continue for Mrs. Bentley. The Court of Appeal for British Columbia just affirmed that holding.[61]

A United States court has not yet interpreted the effect of a Living Will that calls for no spoon feeding once the patient requires prompting or pushes away the hand that feeds him. In the meantime, each Living Will declarant needs to consider his views on whether to include dementia-type triggers in his written advance directive. If he chooses to do so, medical and basic care instructions in the event of that triggering event need to be crystal clear. Odds are a U.S. court will be addressing a similar issue one day in the not too distant future.

> **Lightbulb moment!** In the **For further information** in the back of this book you will find a source for dementia-specific language now available for insertion in a Living Will, or you may choose to have a lawyer draft a clause that works better for you. Be very specific about what you hope to accomplish so that precise language is used that accurately reflects your personal preferences. As you've seen, words truly matter.

That 800-pound gorilla is persistent, you've gotta give him that. Frankly, there are some things you simply cannot plan for. The best approach is to craft written advance directives that reflect personal preferences, incorporate appropriate triggering events and include unambiguous treatment instructions for the physician and proxy.

Withholding vs. withdrawing

One of the most important and least understood legal and ethical concepts is that of withholding (not starting) vs. withdrawing (stopping) treatment. There is no difference, under the law or medical ethics, between withholding and withdrawing a medical procedure and that includes life prolonging measures. With a patient's right to consent to medical treatment comes the right to refuse to consent—and withdraw previously given consent—whether directly or through a proxy. It's well established in court rulings and as stated in the policy of the American Medical Association: "Once initiated, life sustaining treatments may be ethically withdrawn upon request of the patient, or a surrogate or court acting on the patient's behalf."[62]

You may know of a patient or proxy who hesitated to allow the use of a ventilator or feeding tube because he erroneously believed—whether due to his own mistaken thinking or misinformation provided by health care professionals—that the decision was not reversible. True, it may be more emotionally traumatic to withdraw a treatment already in place, but that does not alter the fact that personal freedom permits the refusal of any treatment, including one already begun.[63]

When the potential futility of applying a life prolonging measure is uncertain, a patient or proxy can authorize medical treatment for a "time-limited trial" with the assent of the attending physician. The situation can then be revisited after an agreed upon period of time, and a decision made to continue or withdraw treatment.

Withholding and withdrawing are legally and ethically equivalent.

Lightbulb moment! Now that you are no longer confused about withholding vs. withdrawing, make sure everyone who may be involved with the enforcement of your advance directives has a clear and accurate understanding of this concept as well. It is one of the most frequent regrets I hear from survivors: they didn't understand that a time-limited trial was a possibility for their loved ones. You might be surprised to discover who needs some clarification on this very important subject.

Life prolonging measures

What was commonly called "life support" is now referred to as a "life prolonging" or a "life sustaining" measure. It is medical treatment used to support or replace a primary bodily function. It does not cure or reverse the underlying disease or condition, it simply supplements or replaces a vital spontaneous function, and in its absence, the patient dies.

An important concept is that the use of life prolonging measures is not just for end-of-life medical scenarios; life prolonging measures can be used to keep a patient alive while the underlying medical condition improves (a time-limited trial). Intending to refuse life prolonging procedures as a <u>permanent</u> measure, people often choose Living Will forms with language that excludes their use in <u>all</u> circumstances, temporary or otherwise. This is usually by way of the ever-pointless "I don't want to be a vegetable—no life prolonging measures for me!" clause. Such poorly drafted advance directives can be misleading and confusing for the physician and proxy. Here's a story to illustrate this misguided perception:

Angela suffers from COPD (Chronic Obstructive Pulmonary Disease). She lives independently with the use of an oxygen tank and very little medical intervention most of the time, but she's managed to get pneumonia and is now in intensive care. She's too sick to make decisions for herself or even to understand what's going on around her, so her son Elvin steps in as her appointed health care proxy.

Angela's pulmonary specialist suggests that going on a ventilator would probably help Angela a great deal. He recommends that and asks Elvin what he thinks his mother would want. The doctor waits as Elvin pulls out a copy of his mother's Living Will and reads it over again. Since first getting ill a few years earlier, Angela has been very clear that she doesn't want to live like Mrs. Potato Head—as she puts it—nothing more than a burden on Elvin. Her Living Will says she doesn't wish to have any life prolonging measures such as a ventilator or feeding tube if she is in "a terminal condition that will result in my death in a relatively short period of time or in an irreversible state of permanent unconsciousness." It's crystal clear. Nevertheless, Elvin is confused and, apparently, so is the doctor. Does this mean Elvin's mother wouldn't want him to consent to the ventilator?

Let's first look at whether a triggering event has occurred which should prompt Elvin to refer to the terms of his mother's Living Will. Until the pneumonia crisis, no one considered Angela's COPD a terminal condition that she would die from in a relatively short period of time; she was doing just fine. Actually, her doctor tells Elvin that he thinks antibiotics will address the pneumonia if she can get some help with her breathing. She's definitely not in an irreversible state of permanent unconsciousness.

It's almost as if the doctor and Elvin are reading Angela's Living Will backwards: If a treatment that may prolong her life is being considered, then a triggering event must have occurred, right? This approach suggests that any medical condition that may result in death if not treated (a very liberal definition of "terminal," by the way) should trigger a debate about whether to use the life prolonging treatment in question. That sort of thinking could bar the use of the antibiotics as well. Sometimes a medical treatment is just a medical treatment, even though it can also be a life prolonging measure. In this case, Angela needs the ventilator to help her recover from pneumonia, period.

Elvin and the doctor finally get their heads on straight, and Angela lives to go home after three days on the ventilator. This is an example of why more explanatory directives make a better decision-making tool for the physician and proxy. It's also a good argument for the use of a combination advance directive form, but that's a discussion for another place (Chapter Nine, actually).

Basic life support

First developed in the 1960s, cardiopulmonary resuscitation (CPR), is a form of life support, the most basic form, even though it is not appropriate for long-term use. Consisting of manual chest compressions and mouth-to-mouth breathing, it is the attempt to revive someone who has suffered cardiac arrest (the heart has stopped) and/or respiratory arrest (breathing has stopped). It is also done to keep blood flowing to the person's brain until the heart starts beating again. In a hospital, it can include the use of intubation, respiratory equipment, intravenous resuscitation drugs and an automated external defibrillator (IED).[64] Unfortunately, CPR has a very low rate of success, much lower than portrayed in television dramas. Less than eight percent of people who suffer cardiac arrest outside a hospital survive.[65] For those hospitalized at the time of treatment, 11.6-18.7 percent survive to be discharged.[66] The significance of CPR in a discussion of life prolonging measures is most pertinent to Do Not Resuscitate orders, a little further on in this chapter.

Mechanical ventilation

When a person cannot breathe unaided due to pulmonary disease, an upper spinal cord injury, a neurological disease or a brain injury, mechanical ventilation (a ventilator) can be used. A ventilator is a tube inserted in the nose or mouth or directly into the windpipe to force air into the lungs. It is important to understand that just because the use of a ventilator is suggested does not necessarily mean the patient has a terminal or even an irreversible condition. A ventilator can also be used for short-term assistance, whether or not the patient's underlying disease is terminal.

Artificial nutrition and hydration

If a patient cannot be fed by mouth (oral feeding), artificial nutrition and hydration (a feeding tube) may be an option. Liquids are delivered by a tube entering the digestive system through the nose, mouth, wall of the stomach or intestine. Or an intravenous line is placed into a vein for hydration and short term nutrition. Putting aside for a moment any cultural or religious objections to the withholding or withdrawal of artificial nutrition and hydration, legally speaking, artificial nutrition and hydration is a medical procedure. It must be consented to by the patient or his proxy and can be withdrawn once begun.

As with any other health care decision, the burdens of tubal feeding must be weighed against its benefits. Patients in a permanent vegetative state with no underlying terminal disease can live for many years as long as their nutritional needs are met. However, for a person actively dying or with late-stage dementia, tubal feeding may or may not extend life. In America, where feeding is often associated with nurturing, it may be difficult to understand that for a dying patient whose metabolic system is winding down, a decreased appetite is to be expected and the administration of nutrition, orally or artificially, can actually cause discomfort. In fact, tubal feeding may be a source of diminished quality of life if it requires the patient to be restrained or sedated. There is also the potential for medical complications from tubal feeding, such as nausea, aspiration and infection.

In cases where continued feeding is appropriate, more intense assisted oral feeding (spoon feeding) may provide the necessary nutritional requirements for a patient who can still safely swallow, although it has the practical disadvantage of being labor intensive and time-consuming for caregivers.[67] Keep in mind that assisted oral feeding is not generally considered medical care but rather personal care or basic care—it is not "artificial nutrition" as that term is used in most written advance directives.

Even if a patient has a written advance directive containing a dementia-related trigger, a health care provider or care facility may not agree to withhold nutrition and hydration by any method—in spite of what's clearly stated in the patient's Living Will. Patients have rights but institutions have policies.

> **Lightbulb moment!** If you, as a patient or as the proxy for another, have specific concerns about a care facility's policy on spoon feeding and feeding tubes, inquire at the time of admission. Or, if you are in the preliminary stages of previewing facilities, be sure to ask ahead of time. And get it in writing.

In 13 states, for artificial nutrition and/or hydration to be withheld or withdrawn, the patient's written advance directive must include an unambiguous instruction to forego that life prolonging measure (think *Cruzan*). See **For further information** for sources to check your state's law.

Kidney dialysis

It's the job of the kidneys (most people have two) to remove excess fluids, minerals and wastes from our blood. If kidney failure results from chronic kidney disease and a transplant is not an option or not yet available, dialysis is used to remove wastes and extra salt and liquids. Most people undergo dialysis three times a week. For acute kidney failure, it is possible to use short-term dialysis, but that is not typical.[68]

Almost 26 million Americans have some degree of chronic kidney disease, and more than a half million people are currently on dialysis. The voluntary decision to withdraw from dialysis is made by twenty to twenty-five percent of dialysis patients,[69] and depending on an individual's general health condition, a patient can live from one to several weeks after treatment is discontinued.

Medical treatments

Living Wills focus on issues associated with the end of life, but many times the medical decisions made by patients and proxies involve care that is less dramatic—but just as important—as The Big Three life prolonging measures. Medical decision making may be required anywhere along the health care continuum, and sometimes what begins as a routine medical procedure can unexpectedly and rapidly evolve into a critical care or even an end-of-life crisis.

Available treatment options are more abundant now than ever before. There are broad spectrum antibiotics, chemotherapy, radiation, surgical procedures, blood transfusions, advanced wound treatment, sophisticated imaging equipment, oxygen masks, pacemakers and implantable cardioverter defibrillators (ICDs). Not technically "life prolonging," perhaps these medical procedures should be labeled "life extending" because the withholding or withdrawal of one or more can cause death to come sooner, rather than later. Just as important, any one of them can serve as palliative or comfort care for the patient and, as such, may have the unintended effect of prolonging the patient's life, even though they aren't intended to cure or replace a vital bodily function.

More treatment options necessitate more decision making by the patient or his proxy. Keep in mind that any medical treatment should be consented to with one or more of these identifiable purposes in mind:

- To cure the underlying disease.
- To treat symptoms, without an intent to cure.
- To prolong the patient's life.
- To provide palliative or comfort care.

It's possible that a medical procedure will prolong the process of dying rather than extend life, if one can grasp the subtle difference. Here's an example from a friend whose father recently passed away. Over a period of hours, he went from living independently to being acutely ill with pneumonia. Everyone agreed to the insertion of a mechanical ventilator, but when it became clear he had a very short time to live, he asked that it be removed so he could talk to his family, gathered at his bedside. The ventilator was serving only to prolong the dying process and delay the inevitable. Her father made that decision—which his loved ones accepted—knowing it might hasten his death to some degree. It was an acceptable trade-off because it allowed him to spend his remaining time without the restrictive presence of the ventilator. He had things he wanted and needed to say.

Here's another example. Each month more than 10,000 people in America receive an implantable cardioverter defibrillator (ICD), which may also include a pacemaker. It returns the heart to a normal rhythm: if the heart beats too slowly, the pacemaker sends tiny electrical signals to the heart; if the heart beats too fast or irregularly, it delivers defibrillation shocks to restore a normal rhythm.[70] That's fine for the patient with a life-threatening heart condition who, just a few years ago, would have had no treatment options. However, for the 20 to 25 percent of dying ICD patients who receive an unwelcome and pointless shock from their device within weeks of death, it is not a blessing.[71] (An ICD can be disabled with a portable device; no surgery is required.)

Life extending medical treatment may be the right choice or it may not be worth the trade-off. If the patient or proxy and health care professionals agree that palliative care rather than cure is the treatment goal, the use—or continued use—of a medical treatment can then be evaluated with that objective in mind.

Lightbulb moment! As the patient or proxy, it's important to have a written record of medications, allergies and existing medical conditions. In emergencies, that information can avoid potential drug interactions and medical treatment conflicts; in end-of-life care, prescriptions or medical devices (such as diuretics or an ICD) that no longer serve a treatment purpose may cause discomfort or negative side effects for the patient. This should be addressed during the hospital or hospice admissions process.

Palliative care

Palliative care focuses on relieving the symptoms of a disease or disorder without any intent to cure. That doesn't mean palliative care is only appropriate once a disease is incurable; palliative care can be for the symptoms of a disease or even the side effects of treatment such as chemotherapy or radiation. Palliative care is meant to comfort the patient and provide the highest possible quality of life.

Are you wondering why the issue of palliative care should be covered in your advance directives? Why do you need a directive that tells your physician and proxy to keep you comfortable and pain-free? Shouldn't that be instinctive for them? Even assuming it will be, communicating specifics about your preferences can assist in proxy decision making as well as in personalizing your care.

Pain Management

The four vital signs routinely monitored in a patient are body temperature, pulse rate, respiration rate (rate of breathing) and blood pressure. A fifth vital sign has been recognized in recent years, an aspect of any medical condition that can adversely affect all others: patient pain. What began in hospice care and is now part of general pain management is the realization that there is more than one type of pain. The concept of "total pain" was originally proposed by Dr. Cicely Saunders, the British physician who is considered the founder of modern hospice care. She noted that her patients' pain had emotional, social and spiritual—as well as physical—roots. Dr. Saunders advocated for ways to address patients' anxiety over the issues surrounding end of life and pioneered the concept that mental and physical pain are interdependent.

Tolerance for pain is unique to each patient, and suffering should not be accepted as a "natural" and inevitable part of the dying process—it is not. The role of pain management in advance health care planning lies in the importance of sharing with loved ones ahead of time any fears you may have about suffering at life's end, whether due to physical pain or fear-based anxiety. A patient may hesitate to ask for sufficient pain relief because he feels his last bit of control is being relinquished; another may fear building up resistance that will diminish relief "when I really need it." Viewing pain management with a palliative care perspective means considering treatment options other than just the right dosage of the right drug. For instance, if it seems strange to be talking about radiation for a hospice patient, it isn't, when you know it can effectively reduce the pain caused by some tumors.[72]

For intractable pain, patients can be fully sedated; that's called "palliative sedation," "terminal sedation" or "sedation to unconsciousness." It is used as a last resort for otherwise unendurable pain when nothing else works, and it may result in the patient being unconscious at the time of death.[73] (The intent of terminal sedation is to relieve pain and should never be confused with euthanasia, which is the intentional taking of a life to relieve suffering.) It will help health care professionals and the proxy in decision making if your directives reflect your opinion on the importance of being conscious at the end of your life.

One of the most common reasons for the undertreatment of pain in the dying is the fear that sufficient pain medication will hasten death, the "principle of double effect." Simply put, the principle states that bad results can sometimes come from good intentions. It goes like this: 1) the intentional act must be good or not morally bad (giving pain medication); 2) the good effect cannot be obtained through the bad effect (pain relief by dying); 3) the bad effect cannot be the intended effect (pain medication is not given to cause death); and 4) the bad effect cannot outweigh the good effect (reducing the unbearable pain outweighs any slight risk of hastening death).[74] Besides the issue of pain relief in the dying, you can see how this principle applies to the practice of surgery and even cancer treatments: the surgeon or oncologist's actions can cause pain, possibly even death, but they are done with the good intent of treating or curing an injury or disease.

It may not be necessary to analyze end-of-life pain relief under the principle of double effect because, in spite of pervasive myths even among medical professionals, there is little real evidence that end-of-life pain medication hastens death. There is, in fact, ample evidence that patients who get higher doses of opioids (morphine-like drugs) live longer than those receiving lower doses.[75] That may be because pain is such an intense stressor on the human body. Regardless, when the sole intent of giving pain medication is the relief of suffering and not to kill the patient, any remote occurrence of hastening death is not euthanasia.

Being an informed patient—or an informed proxy/advocate—will enable you to seek out and engage palliative care specialists with the expertise you need. Once in a medical or end-of-life situation, patient or proxy should be prepared to ask whatever questions are necessary to fully understand the burdens and benefits of specific pain management options. Meaningful advance directives that address pain management give health care providers and the proxy permission to make choices that respect the dying patient's autonomous right to comfort and dignity.

Hospice care

Although Chapter Six is devoted to the subject of hospice care, it's mentioned here because—make no mistake about it—hospice is medical care, not giving up or hopelessness or assigning a "No Treatment" code to the patient. Once it's determined that cure is no longer an option or the patient chooses to discontinue curative treatments for a terminal condition, hospice care should be considered along with other options. Unfortunately, hospice care is often not begun until it's too late to be of optimal value. If you want to make hospice part of your end-of-life care plan, please express that wish now in your advance directives.

Do Not Resuscitate orders (DNRs)

Cardiopulmonary resuscitation (CPR) is used to revive someone whose breathing and/or heart has stopped. In hospital speak, it's a "Full Code." About the time *Last things first, just in case* . . . was published in 2006, the *Des Moines Register* ran a story about an eighty-year-old Iowa woman who didn't want CPR under any circumstances. As a matter of fact, she felt so strongly about it that she had "DO NOT RESUSCITATE" tattooed on her chest.[76] Now, while getting inked may have checked an item off the Bucket List of Mary Wohlford of Dyersville, Iowa, in the event of a cardiac or respiratory emergency, it would have been completely ineffective in preventing CPR. In the same way, Maxine's daughter Wendy thought she could just show her mother's Living Will to the EMSs and they would not attempt to resuscitate her. Mary and Wendy were both wrong for a couple of reasons.

A Do Not Resuscitate order, or DNR (sometimes called a DNAR for Do Not Attempt Resuscitation) is a medical order authorized by a doctor (or a certified nurse practitioner or physician's assistant in some jurisdictions) specifying that resuscitation is not to be attempted in the event of cardiac or respiratory arrest. It is a hospital "No Code." A written advance directive is not a DNR. And, for the record, neither is a tattoo. There is no such thing as a patient- or proxy-issued DNR. A person's Living Will may state that the declarant wants to avoid CPR or to have a DNR issued when and if the time comes, but either one is merely a cue for the physician and proxy to have the necessary medical order written. Once that's done, the proxy should verify visible documentation in the patient's chart, place an identifying notification bracelet on the patient and post a visible sign near the patient's bed.

If cardiac or respiratory arrest occurs when there is no written DNR or the attending physician has not previously determined that attempted resuscitation is not in the patient's best interest, the patient should receive full medical treatment—including CPR. Similarly, if a person with a DNR starts having trouble breathing, he should still receive medical assistance, up until the time his breathing or heart stops. DNR is not the same as "Do Not Treat" or "Comfort Care Only." Every patient, regardless of his DNR status, should receive medical and palliative care in accordance with the goals of his overall treatment plan.

As stated earlier, the survival rate from CPR is not good, especially for elderly or seriously ill persons. In evaluating whether to obtain a DNR, the patient or proxy should have a frank discussion with the attending physician about the advisability of CPR, including the potential negative impact of attempted resuscitation. All parties should understand that the patient can suffer broken ribs or may be revived with brain damage resulting from a lack of oxygen. A physician does not have an ethical responsibility to authorize CPR when he believes it to be futile or not in the patient's best interest.[77]

 **Lightbulb moment!** Without question, confusion between the meaning of DNR orders vs. Living Wills is the number one subject I have been asked about by readers and class attendees. Research studies confirm the dangerous level of misunderstanding among health care professionals, and I've witnessed it firsthand. When you or a loved one are in a hospital setting, make sure everyone is on the same page when it comes to the patient's resuscitation code status. Don't take anything for granted.

On the other hand, if a patient or proxy wants to ensure that resuscitation will be attempted, an unambiguous discussion with the attending physician is also in order. Make sure the appropriate instruction is placed in the patient's record and there is no DNR on file.

If you think this is all a bit confusing, you're not alone.

In a series of studies, medical professionals (emergency medical services, nurses and physicians) were asked to assign a treatment status "code" to a fictitious patient identified as having a Living Will. A staggering majority of the EMS's, nurses and physicians equated having a Living Will with having a DNR ("No Code"). That's very wrong. Worse than that, when the health care professionals were then told that the imaginary patient actually has a physician's DNR, only about a third of respondents knew that DNR patients should still receive full treatment in all other aspects of their medical care, unless otherwise indicated. The overwhelming majority thought a patient with a DNR should receive end-of-life care only.[78]

Those are some scary results. It is a giant leap in the wrong direction to mistakenly believe that because someone has a Living Will, he should be denied medical care if he starts having a heart attack. Or that if he has a Do Not Resuscitate order and breaks his arm, he can expect comfort care only. So the good news is, the patients in those studies were imaginary. The bad news is, the medical professionals who responded so inappropriately are not. If you hadn't yet figured out that knowledge can be a matter of life and death—as a patient or as a proxy—hopefully, you now have.

Out of Hospital-Do Not Resuscitate orders (OOH-DNRs)

Once a patient is discharged from the hospital, a DNR order issued during hospitalization is no longer effective. For someone who wants to avoid attempted resuscitation outside the hospital setting—like the tattooed lady of Dyersville, Iowa—the solution may be an Out of Hospital-Do Not Resuscitate order. Almost all states provide for some version of an OOH-DNR. The criteria vary widely, so check on your state's law. One may require that a person first be classified as terminal while another state may require an estimated life expectancy below a specified maximum before an OOH-DNR can be issued. If Maxine had had an OOH-DNR, Wendy could have shown it to the EMSs, and that would have been the end of that—and Maxine.

Anyone with an OOH-DNR should keep copies of the order handy as well as wear any identifying bracelet or necklace required by law. An OOH-DNR does not mean "Do Not Treat." The person should receive appropriate medical treatment other than attempted resuscitation, and comfort care should always be provided by emergency personnel, even if nothing can be done medically.

Lightbulb moment! Because it usually requires some degree of a "terminal" diagnosis, an OOH-DNR isn't practical for someone who is simply older, frail or just has strong feelings about not being resuscitated. I'm afraid there's little to be done about that. (Unless Mary Wohlford of Dyersville, Iowa had a terminal condition in 2006 that we were not made aware of, she did not qualify for an OOH-DNR in Iowa.) Let's face it, it's unrealistic to expect loved ones—never mind a passing stranger—to <u>not</u> call 9-1-1 in an emergency. Instead, address the issue of further life prolonging measures in your Living Will, in case the CPR works.

POLST (Physician Orders for Life Sustaining Treatment) forms

In 1991, medical ethicists in Oregon concluded that patients' written advance directives were not entirely effective because of their "frequent lack of availability when needed, their lack of clinical specificity with respect to the here-and-now medical decisions faced by seriously ill patients and their lack of integration into medical orders."[79] They devised the Physician Orders for Life Sustaining Treatment (POLST) form. A POLST-type form contains specific and actionable medical orders relating to cardiopulmonary resuscitation; medical interventions, such as antibiotics, hospitalization or "Comfort Measures Only"; and artificial nutrition and hydration.

The stated intentions of the National POLST Paradigm Task Force (NPPTF) are that the form complements—but does not replace—advance directives for persons suffering from a serious illness or frailty with a life expectancy of a year or less. The POLST form is a set of medical orders executed by the patient or his proxy and a doctor, physician's assistant or certified nurse practitioner.[80] It is portable and intended to travel with the patient to the hospital, a nursing facility, hospice or personal residence. To be easily located and recognizable, it's printed on brightly colored paper.

A POLST-type form is not an advance directive. The orders of a POLST may or may not be in alignment with the terms of the patient's advance directives, and it can be authorized by a patient who still has capacity or by a proxy if the patient is no longer competent. Twenty-six states' POLST programs have achieved the status of either "endorsed" or "mature" from the NPPFT. An additional nineteen states are in the process of "developing" a POLST program, which means they are somewhere between simply exploring the idea to fully implementing it through state statutes, medical board regulations or voluntary compliance. States use various labels in addition to "POLST," such as MOLST, POST, COLST or MOST.

One of the stated goals of the POLST movement was to have "standardized medical orders."[81] The founders of the movement believe that a major obstacle to ensuring that patients' wishes are honored is the variability of states' advance directive laws. Well, welcome to the club. There is wide disparity between state POLST-type programs as to elements of the form, what constitutes a qualifying medical condition, execution requirements, and—most important—whether a patient's advance directives are rendered moot by a POLST-type form.[82] In spite of these inconsistencies, each and every one of these state programs is characterized as an NPPTF-sanctioned POLST program.

By now you know the drill: check with the resources in the back of this book to see if there is a POLST-type program in your state and how it may impact the enforceability of your advance directives—verbal and written. Depending on the parameters of the program, you may wish to include in your written advance directives any preferences as to the use or avoidance of a POLST-type form.

The National POLST Paradigm allows "facilitators" (e.g., nurses, social workers, clergy, nursing home administrators) to counsel a patient or proxy on the medical and legal implications of using a POLST-type form. However, common sense and medical ethics dictate that any discussion that may conclude with the giving of informed consent concerning life prolonging measures should only be done with the patient's attending physician serving as the primary source of information. As your end of life approaches, either you or your health care proxy—whether he is appointed in your advance directive or serves as a proxy-by-statute—can and should consult with your physician on a real-time basis to consider your preferences and goals, formulate a treatment plan and authorize appropriate medical orders to implement that plan.

Physician-assisted suicide

Physician-assisted suicide is a doctor legally facilitating death by providing the means or information to enable someone to commit suicide, typically by authorizing a prescription for a lethal dose of medication.[83] Oregon (1997), Washington (2008) and Vermont (2013) have passed state laws legalizing physician-assisted suicide, and Montana (2009) has declared it legal by court decision.[84] As of this writing, the appeal of a court ruling that struck down the New Mexico ban on physician-assisted suicide is pending in the New Mexico Court of Appeals.[85] In 1997, the U.S. Supreme Court held in twin cases that a state's prohibition of assisted suicide is not a violation of the Equal Protection Clause; that the distinction between letting a patient die and making that patient die is important, logical, rational and well established; and that there is no right to commit suicide.[86] Not coincidentally, while the conjoined *Vacco* and *Glucksberg* cases were pending in front of the U.S. Supreme Court, President Clinton signed the Assisted Suicide Funding Restriction Act of 1997 into law. The Act prohibits the use of federal funds to pay for assisted suicide or euthanasia. This ban extends to Medicaid, Medicare, military and veterans' health care and any other federally-funded health care services.[87]

The Oregon, Washington and Vermont statutes are virtually identical. The person must be at least 18 years of age, he must be certified by two physicians to be competent and to have a terminal diagnosis of six months or less to live, he must self-administer the drug and he must be a resident of the state. The physician writes a prescription to be dispensed by a pharmacy. In Oregon, prescriptions have been written for 1,173 patients, and 752 have died after taking the prescribed drug since 1997.[88] From 2009-2013 in Washington, 547 prescriptions were written; 359 died after ingesting the drug.[89] Consistently in both Oregon and Washington and for all years since legalization, the reasons cited by patients seeking physician-assisted suicide are loss of autonomy, decreasing ability to participate in activities that made life enjoyable and loss of dignity, in that order. Inadequate pain control or the fear of its inevitability comes in at sixth on the lists.

As of this writing, 26 states have introduced legislation in either 2014 or 2015 to legalize physician-assisted suicide.[90]

Euthanasia and assisted suicide

For many, hearing the term "physician-assisted suicide" brings Jack Kevorkian to mind. A former Michigan doctor, Kevorkian claimed to have assisted over 130 people in dying, the last one being Thomas Youk, a 52-year-old suffering from Lou Gehrig's disease. Kevorkian, whose license to practice medicine had been revoked in 1991, was shown giving a fatal injection to Youk on videotape, telecast on CBS's "60 minutes" on November 22, 1998. Strictly speaking, it was not "physician-assisted suicide," because Jack Kevorkian was not a physician at the time. And since he was the direct cause of Thomas Youk's death by lethal injection, it also wasn't suicide. In later writings, Kevorkian himself labeled it as "medical euthanasia," and according to the state of Michigan, it was second-degree murder. Jack Kevorkian was convicted in 1999 and sentenced to 10-25 years in prison.[91] He served eight years and died of natural causes on June 3, 2011.[92]

What used to be known as "mercy killing" is now referred to as euthanasia. It is the act of killing or bringing about the death of a person who suffers from an incurable disease or condition. It is not legal anywhere in the United States, and the act is classified throughout the states as criminal homicide of some degree.

Lightbulb moment! Just across the northern border of the United States, Canada's Supreme Court very recently ruled that the Canadian ban on both physician-assisted suicide and physician-assisted euthanasia are unconstitutional. It will be a teachable moment for the United States to observe Parliament's legislative response to that decision (the ruling's effect is delayed for one year while Canadian lawmakers adopt procedural safeguards to implement the legalization of these acts—or not.)

Suicide with the assistance of someone <u>other</u> <u>than</u> a physician is illegal by statute or common law throughout the United States, except for Nevada, North Carolina, Utah and Wyoming, where the legal status is unclear. In the other 47 jurisdictions, the criminal charge is either manslaughter, a felony or murder.[93] (Physician-assisted suicide, as you now know, is legal in four states as of this writing.)

Why should a discussion of care options include acts that are not legal? Because it's important to understand that it serves no real purpose to have directives, verbal or in writing, that would subject a physician or proxy to criminal prosecution. Rash statements such as "just kill me if that happens" do nothing to give caregivers the realistic instructions they need in order to honor the patient's autonomy.

Organ donation

In 1967, the first successful heart transplant was performed in the United States. Now each day an average of 79 people receive an organ transplant as another 21 die waiting for a donor. There are currently 79,921 qualified candidates on the national organ transplant waiting list.[94] Much of this discussion about death and dying has focused on older Americans, and a common mistaken belief is that advanced age automatically disqualifies one from being an organ donor. Actually, 35.3 percent of the deceased donors in 2013 were 50 years of age and older,[95] and organ donation may even be an option for hospice patients, depending on the cause of death. Organ donation is another item to be addressed in a written advance directive.

If you wish to be an organ donor, first enter your name in your state's donor registry. When a person fails to pre-register, next of kin are sometimes uncomfortable granting permission because they're uncertain of the donor's wishes, don't understand that organ donation does not disfigure the body in any way or think the family is responsible for costs associated with donation. The procurement procedure does require the deceased's body to be removed immediately upon death, but arrangements can be made for the family to be with their loved one's body once that process is completed. Whether or not specified in your Living Will, instruct your loved ones to consent to organ donation, if it is feasible.

If a person does <u>not</u> want to be an organ donor upon death, based on a religious objection or for any other reason, that should be verbally communicated and clearly stated in the Living Will, to prevent the proxy or family members from consenting against the patient's wishes.

Donated organs, eyes and tissue are harvested from a person declared brain dead who continues to breathe with the use of a ventilator (the "dead donor rule") or from a person who has suffered cardiopulmonary death and has been determined to be in "irreversible" cardiac and respiratory failure ("organ donation after cardiac death").[96] For many people, both circumstances prompt ethical questions. It may be difficult to understand that a person diagnosed as brain dead is medically dead. Likewise, when is it ethical to stop resuscitation attempts and rule a person's condition "irreversible" so the removal of organs can commence?[97] No easy answers to be found here.

Under the law, if a patient has registered as an organ donor and/or specified his wish to be a donor in written directives, that consent cannot be withheld by survivors.[98] That may or may not jibe with reality simply because health care professionals are unlikely to get into a clash with determined survivors. However, the patient's intent—whatever that may be—previously expressed verbally and in written directives can be critical to ensuring survivors' peace of mind and to having the patient's wishes honored.

Lightbulb moment! If you have any interest in being an organ donor, check out your state's organ registry, and if you decide to proceed, register online or by mail, specify that status in your written advance directives, carry a donor card and make the proper notation the next time you renew your driver's license. The easier you make it for your survivors to consent, the more likely your wishes will be honored.

Other advance planning choices

Complex life prolonging treatment choices tend to cloud the vision when trying to picture what the dying process might be like. But simpler things can also play a key role in honoring a person's end-of-life preferences. Once the treatment plan and caregivers are focused on palliative care, the four elements of total pain—emotional, social, spiritual and physical—should be kept in mind. Consider if any of these preferences are ones you'd like to include in your advance directives:

- If a choice is possible, where would you prefer to die?
- Do you want someone with you as death approaches, and, if so, who?
- Is there a special quilt, photo, pillow or other item you want nearby?
- Do you want to listen to music or watch television or movies?
- Would you like someone to read to you. And, if so, what?
- Do you have a preference about whether you have visitors or who visits?
- Do you want assistance in looking your best for visitors?
- Is it important that you be able to observe religious traditions?
- Do you want someone close by to hold your hand?
- If you have pets, would you like them nearby if possible?
- Is there anywhere special you would like to be, such as near a window?
- Would you like the opportunity to leave special messages for loved ones by having someone transcribe your words or make a tape recording or video?

When you think of the people, daily rituals and even objects that bring you joy, consider including them in your end-of-life plan. Just as in everyday life, as death approaches, it is often the little things that nurture a person's spirit and offer the most comfort. Dying is part of living and life is a jewel with many facets.

The disposition of remains

Think about it: putting together a funeral or memorial service is like being expected to plan an event on the scale of a wedding with practically no lead time. Much of that anxiety can be eliminated for loved ones by considering, discussing and recording wishes for a service, if any. Preplanning can be as informal as leaving a list of songs and readings and noting burial or cremation preferences. Or it can be as formal as meeting with a funeral director or planner to put detailed instructions in writing and paying for it all ahead of time.

Some state laws dictate who has legal authority to make decisions regarding the disposition of a body and the legal effect of the deceased's written or oral instructions. They may require the use of a specific form for directives or to designate a surrogate decision maker for cremation, burial, cryogenics (for real) or ritual decisions. (Refer back to Chapter Four under "The proxy's role after the principal's death" for additional information.) To see how one state's legislators have taken the position that the very last person who should decide how to dispose of the deceased is the deceased, check out *In re: The estate of Mary Florence Whalen, Deceased. Michael Whalen, Appellant*, courtesy of the Iowa Supreme Court. It's a doozy.[99]

If it matters to you what happens to your earthly vessel after you're gone, you should take steps to record your preferences. If it's a nonissue for you, then let your family and friends know that and give them permission to do whatever will bring comfort to them. In any case, your loved ones will thank you for any forethought and preplanning that you do. As with many matters relating to the end of life, knowing you are carrying out a loved one's wishes is equally beneficial as being relieved of the burden of decision making.

Lightbulb moment! Visit the sources shown in **For further information** to learn more about your options for funeral or memorial services, on any budget. True, you won't be here to enjoy it (unless you think you might be), but respecting your loved ones means helping as much as possible to communicate your preferences while you still are.
You know what would be an awesome gift for your survivors? Your obituary, composed by the person who knows you best. Who better to decide what to put in and what to leave out? Do you want future generations to learn about your professional history or is your ethical legacy more important to you? As for the accomplishments you're most proud of, only you can name them. Think about it.

Medical futility in end-of-life care

A 2013 Pew Research survey indicates that the percentage of people who believe there are circumstances where medical staff should "always do everything possible to save the life of a patient in all circumstances" has increased from 15 percent in 1990 to 31 percent in 2013. What do you suppose that implies? Perhaps some of the increase comes from fewer people having no opinion on the matter (that's down 9 percent from 1990).[100] Or do more people now recognize that the theoretical patient on the gurney could one day soon be them? Or maybe, just maybe, it's that they don't really understand what "everything" means. That leads into the subject of "medical futility" and, in fairness, a discussion of treatment options is not complete without it. The 800-pound gorilla known as "When is enough enough?" is difficult to ignore.

Medical futility is not so easy to define because one has to consider the patient's or proxy's purpose or intent in consenting to a treatment, the effort and expense involved and sometimes no more than a health care professional's best guess on the chances for success. Ethically, a physician does not have an obligation to provide care that, in his opinion, does not have a reasonable chance of benefiting the patient and altering the patient's ultimate clinical outcome.[101] So, as it turns out, patients don't really have the power to demand that "everything" be done, but, hey, as long as the health care system is willing to assent, patients and proxies keep asking.

Until and unless the patient, proxy and physician first discuss the patient's goals—treatment and personal—for his remaining life, gauging the futility of any one particular treatment or procedure is virtually impossible. For instance, CPR for a dying patient appears to be the consummate example of medical futility, doesn't it? Not if that patient's only remaining goal is to stay alive long enough to see and say goodbye to the last family member yet to arrive. Ideally, the issue of futility is addressed through a shared decision-making process. That's a delicate balancing act of the patient's and proxy's unique values and perspectives, the physician's professional knowledge and the ethical obligations and agendas of all those other bystanders: the patient's many loved ones and the meshing gears of the health care system.

Life—and death—used to be so simple. Not very long ago, as evidenced by the landmark legal cases, you had ventilators and you had feeding tubes. That narrow field of choices greatly reduced the need for tricky decision making, because a ventilator couldn't prolong the life of a patient whose kidneys were rapidly failing, and there was no need to debate the use of a feeding tube for someone with untreatable congestive heart failure. For many decades, the limited parameters of Living Wills worked just fine. Now, in order for this complex health care system to properly function, patient, proxy and physician need to understand medical and legal terminology and—as important—their respective roles in the shared decision-making process.

Chapter review

- Before your physician and loved ones turn to your written advance directives for guidance on the use of life prolonging measures, they need to determine if a "triggering event" has occurred. That has traditionally meant conditions like "a terminal disease" and "a permanent and irreversible state of unconsciousness."

- You will now find Living Will forms that include the unique characteristics of dementia-type diseases as a triggering event.
- There is no legal or ethical difference between withholding and withdrawing a medical treatment, which includes life prolonging measures.
- "Life prolonging" or "life sustaining" measures or procedures refer to medical treatment used to support or replace a primary bodily function without curing or reversing the underlying condition.
- Cardiopulmonary resuscitation, first developed in the 1960s, is a form of life support—the most basic form—and is not appropriate for long-term use.
- When a person cannot breathe unaided due to pulmonary disease, an upper spinal cord injury, a neurological disease or a brain injury, a ventilator can be used for long-term or short-term assistance.
- If a patient cannot be fed by mouth (oral feeding), artificial nutrition and hydration (a feeding tube) may be an option. As with any other health care decision, the burdens of tubal feeding must be weighed against its benefits.
- If kidney failure occurs and a transplant is not an option or not available, dialysis filters the patient's blood through a dialyzer to remove wastes and extra salt and liquids.
- Any medical treatment should be consented to with one or more of these identifiable purposes in mind: 1) to cure the underlying disease, 2) in a continuing effort to treat the disease, without an intent to cure, 3) to prolong the patient's life or 4) to provide palliative or comfort care.
- Palliative care focuses on relieving symptoms without the intent to cure for those suffering from the effects of any disease or even from the side effects of a medical treatment.
- A fifth vital sign has been recognized in recent years, an element of the patient's condition that can adversely affect all others: patient pain.
- Once it is determined that cure is no longer an option, the use of hospice care should be evaluated along with other medical treatments.
- If a hospitalized person does not wish to have CPR performed, a written Do Not Resuscitate order (DNR) must be issued by a health care professional.
- Almost all states provide for some version of an Out of Hospital-Do Not Resuscitate order (OOH-DNR).
- Unlike an advance directive, a POLST-type form (Physician Orders for Life Sustaining Treatment) provides actionable medical orders.
- Physician-assisted suicide is a doctor legally facilitating death by providing the means or information to enable someone to commit suicide, typically by authorizing a prescription for a lethal dose of medication. It is legal in four states.
- Euthanasia is killing or bringing about the death of a person who suffers from an incurable disease or condition. It is illegal throughout the United States.

- Loved ones should be made aware of your preference for being an organ, tissue and eye donor. If you do wish to be a donor, you should enter your name in your state's donor registry as well as specifying that in your written directives.
- Personal choices concerning one's environment at the end of life can be included in conversations about care wishes and in written advance directives.
- If you have preferences about the disposition of your body after death, learn about your state's relevant law and then discuss and properly record your wishes.
- Ethically, a physician does not have an obligation to provide medically futile care that, in his opinion, does not have a reasonable chance of benefiting the patient and altering the patient's ultimate clinical outcome.

Chapter Six
Hospice and palliative care

While I thought that I was learning how to live,
I have been learning how to die.
Leonardo da Vinci

The term "dysfunctional" probably wouldn't be used to describe a seriously messed up family nearly a century ago, but in 1918 that's exactly where the little girl finds herself. A wealthy home, yes, but more vividly marked by unhappiness, chaos and feuding adults. There's a contentious divorce, a custody battle, even abandonment. And if that isn't enough, she is born with a congenital back defect, a crooked spine that causes her intense and lifelong physical and emotional pain. And so begins a journey of struggles and triumphs for the child named Cicely.

As a young woman, she defies her father's wishes by dropping out of college when World War II begins to pursue her dream of being a nurse, then has to quit when her back issues become unbearable. Undeterred, Cicely takes training as a medical social worker. That's when she first finds her deep faith and discovers a compelling passion: care for the dying. Relieving patients' physical discomfort seems an obvious and critical priority to Cicely, but what of the social, emotional and spiritual elements of what patients often describe to her as "overall misery"? Her frustration with the medical profession's ignorance of the unique patient issues surrounding life's end leads her to become a physician at age forty. Dr. Cicely Saunders is finally able to give full attention to what she comes to label "total pain."

In 1967, Dr. Saunders opens St. Christopher's Hospice in London, England. Hospice-like institutions had existed throughout the centuries; the first hospices were founded in the Middle Ages to provide sanctuary for ailing pilgrims travelling to holy shrines, hoping to receive miracle cures. Many did not survive the trip, so places of rest became places of dying. However, it was Dr. Cicely Saunders' revolutionary concept of total pain that transformed shelters for simply dying into the multi-disciplinary practice that has come to be known as modern hospice care.[102]

Meanwhile, across the pond, the dean of the Harvard School of Nursing, Florence Wald, is also facing the frustrations of a lack of physician-patient communication, poor symptom management and the system's failure to recognize the essential role of patient autonomy in the dying process. The lives of Florence and Cicely are marked by similarities and coincidence: Florence Wald also suffers from a severe childhood ailment, she overcomes paternal resistance to be a nurse and then, by chance, attends a lecture at Harvard in 1963. The speaker? Dr. Cicely Saunders. She has come from

England to learn more about pain management from her American counterparts. Not long after that seminal event, Florence Wald resigns as dean and devotes the remainder of her life to advocacy for the dying. Along with two pediatricians and a chaplain, she opens Connecticut Hospice, the first American hospice program. The year is 1974.

Hospice is a philosophy

Hospice is an interdisciplinary approach to patient care when a cure is no longer possible or a patient chooses to discontinue curative treatment. It focuses on the dying patient's overall comfort, addressing his "total pain." For the patient, the ultimate treatment goal in hospice care is to live as well as possible—as defined by the patient directly or through his proxy—until natural death comes. Along with addressing physical symptoms and pain management, hospice includes spiritual, social and emotional support for the patient and—unlike other health care disciplines—includes the welfare of the patient's loved ones in the treatment plan. Some of the therapies of holistic hospice care are pain relief; massage; physical, speech and occupational therapies; meditation; pastoral and bereavement counseling; and complementary care such as art, aroma, music, pet, Reiki and healing touch therapies.

The medical specialty of palliative care focuses on improving the patient's quality of life by relieving suffering from the treatment of a disease or its side effects, and it has evolved alongside hospice care. (Hospice care always includes a palliative element, but because palliative care may be appropriate at any stage of any illness, introducing palliative care doesn't necessarily mean someone is dying.)

A patient qualifies for Medicare hospice benefits once a physician certifies that the patient has six or fewer months to live, assuming the terminal disease runs its normal course. This is true of most private insurance hospice benefits as well. More than nine of every ten hospice patient days in America are now covered by the Medicare Part A hospice benefit, which has been available since 1982.[103] It pays for all hospice-related physician services or nursing care, pharmaceuticals, medical supplies and equipment and counseling.[104]

The core of the mission of hospice is the conviction that all dying persons are entitled to compassion and dignity, with respect for their personal values and preferences. It is sometimes described as facilitating a patient-defined "good death." In attempting to quantify that concept, the Grattan Institute in Australia has created a list of key issues for dying patients. Some of the universal areas of concern are these: knowing what to expect and when it will happen, control over where death occurs and who is present, dignity and privacy, control over pain relief and symptom management, access to information and spiritual and emotional support, having advance directives that will be respected and not having life needlessly prolonged.[105]

As much as hospice is a blessing for the dying patient who is approaching the end of life, it is equally important for the patient's loved ones and, most especially, those who provide 24/7 care for the patient, sometimes over months, even years. It includes attention to the social, emotional and spiritual needs of the patient's family, caregivers and those present to witness the passing. Hospice supplements the service of caregivers by providing expert end-of-life palliative care and encouraging loved ones to spend precious time with their dying loved one saying whatever remains to be said. That assistance to survivors continues past the time of death to include group and individual grief counseling. Whether the patient remains at home or is able to and chooses to die in a residential hospice facility, caregivers deserve the chance to be supported in their loss, before and after the death of the patient.

Hospice is a place—many places, really

Ten years after Connecticut Hospice opened in 1974, there were 31 Medicare-certified hospices in the United States. Today there are over 5,800. Where is care actually provided? The short answer is, wherever patients are found. Hospice can serve through periodic visits in a hospital, a long-term care facility (nursing home), an assisted living apartment or a private residence. Eighty percent of Americans wish they could die at home but only 25 percent of all Americans do. Those with advance directives are more likely to die in hospice care,[106] and of those under hospice care, 66.6 percent do die at home, so advance directives are serving more than just their defined purpose.[107] As for dying in a hospital, 29 percent of all deaths occur there,[108] but only seven percent of patients in hospice care are hospitalized at the time of death.

Some communities have a freestanding hospice house or rooms in a hospital or long-term care facility reserved for hospice patients. That's where more than a fourth of hospice patients die. Medicare also provides a short-term "respite" benefit that provides inpatient care in a nursing home, residential hospice facility or hospital, allowing the patient's home caregiver to get a brief break.

Hospice is people—lots and lots of people

During 2013, over 1,500,000 people received hospice care in the United States. Over one million died while under hospice care, representing 43 percent of all deaths in America, compared to only 19.4 percent in 1996.[109] No doubt that boost is due both to demographics (an overwhelming percentage of hospice deaths are of older Americans, a group which continues to grow), and to mounting public awareness of the availability and advantages of a hospice-attended end of life. Still, that's quite a leap.

Hospice services are provided by physicians; nurses; hospice aides; home health care aides; social workers; speech, physical, occupational and complementary care therapists; and pastoral, bereavement and grief counselors. Most of the hands-on care of hospice patients, however, is provided by informal caregivers in the home. They are usually family members or close friends and they are usually unpaid. In fact, if all the uncompensated caregivers in this country demanded pay, it would cost about the same as the annual Medicare budget, $641 billion.[110]

Medicare certification requires that at least five percent of patient care hours be provided by volunteers. So let it be written, so let it be done. In 2013, 355,000 hospice volunteers across the nation donated about 16 million hours of their time to everything from fundraising to holding the hand of a dying patient.[111]

Hospice myths and facts

Choosing whether and when to begin hospice care is much like other subjects relating to the end of life: just when you most need facts and clarity to make informed decisions, you're plagued by information overload and confusion. That's why now—while you're calm and capacitated—is a good time to dispel some of the myths surrounding hospice care.

Myth: Hospice care is only for old people or people with cancer.

Fact: It's true that patients with diseases having protracted dying trajectories, like dementia, heart disease, lung disease, stroke and kidney disease, are common in hospice care.[112] That explains why 80 percent of hospice patients are 65 years of age and older. And, yes, cancer patients make up the largest category of primary diagnoses in hospice (36.5 percent), but as seen in the cases of Karen Ann Quinlan, Nancy Cruzan and Theresa Schiavo, ends of life that require and deserve specialized compassionate care befall the young as well as the aging.

Myth: If a patient is in a long-term care facility or hospital and makes the decision to enter hospice care, he has to use the hospice provider the care facility refers him to.

Fact: Patients who qualify for Medicare benefits can go to the Medicare-certified hospice provider of their choice.[113] Choosing a hospice provider should be based on the type and availability of services, results of family evaluation surveys, staff-to-patient ratios and recommendations from family and friends.

Myth: Entering hospice care means everyone has given up and there's no hope.

Fact: Although transferring into hospice care means that curing the disease is no longer a treatment goal, making the choice to seek hospice care is not medical failure. Dying is a natural part and the ultimate end of every life, a condition that deserves the dedicated and specialized treatment provided by hospice and palliative care. Hospice care focuses on the patient's welfare, comfort and dignity, and until death comes, hope continues for the patient to have his best possible remaining days.

Myth: Hospice is meant for the last few days of a person's life, and you go there when you're ready to die.

Fact: Unfortunately, it's true that many patients delay hospice intervention until pain relief or caregiving becomes unmanageable. In fact, 34.5 percent of hospice patients either die or are discharged within seven days of admission, and the median time spent in hospice care is 18.5 days (half the patients are there for less time, half for more).[114] The fact is that the longer a patient is under hospice care, the more time there is to customize treatment and help the patient achieve his goals for the rest of his life. For family and friends, earlier involvement with hospice can provide the emotional and care support they need and allow them to spend more quality time with their dying loved one. Remember that Medicare provides an unlimited timeline of benefits, as long as certification of less than six-months' life expectancy continues, so care can be augmented in stages as the patient's condition progresses. Deciding whether hospice is appropriate is more of a process than a moment in time, a process that should be guided by the patient's health care professionals through physician-patient-proxy shared decision making.

Myth: If the patient doesn't die within six months, he has to leave hospice care.

Fact: Initial Medicare hospice certification is for two 90-day benefit periods, followed by unlimited 60-day periods, as long as the doctor continues to certify the likelihood of death within six months. There is no "time limit" per se.[115]

Myth: Being in hospice care is the same as having "Do Not Treat" or "Comfort Care Only" medical orders.

Fact: There is no such assumption and "Do Not Treat" is not a legitimate care status code, since that means a medical condition, such as pain, would not be treated with palliative care. Once in hospice, the life-limiting disease or condition is no longer addressed with cure in mind, but the patient does receive palliative care for its symptoms. The patient may also receive medical treatment for conditions other than the disease causing his death. The decision to issue genuine medical orders, such as "Comfort Measures Only," if appropriate, should first be thoroughly discussed by the patient or his proxy and the attending physician.

Myth: Once enrolled in hospice, my loved one's around-the-clock care will be handled by hospice personnel.

Fact: Routine home hospice care provided in a residence consists of periodic visits and evaluation by hospice personnel, as the patient's condition and care needs warrant. For a patient whose level of care becomes complex due to pain management or crisis care issues, full-time hospice staff may be available (continuous home care) or the patient can be moved to a care facility (hospital or nursing home) for inpatient hospice care. If a residential hospice facility is available, the patient can go there to receive all necessary care. Naturally, once the patient is in a care facility or residential hospice facility, basic personal care is provided as well as palliative hospice care.

However, it is <u>very</u> important to understand that hospice care is subject to the same budgetary and staff limitations and human shortcomings as any other component of the health care system. Even though a patient is admitted to continuous or inpatient hospice care, the patient's proxy and loved ones should remain fully engaged in making sure the patient receives the basic care and medical attention he needs and deserves. For instance, if it is the patient's or proxy's wish that the patient not be alone when death comes, there may or may not be hospice volunteers available to serve in that capacity. If not, the proxy and loved ones should arrange for a private-pay attendant or plan to be with the patient in shifts. Likewise, monitoring and providing adequate pain control and comfort is without a doubt the job of the hospice provider, but it remains the duty of the proxy/advocate to see that the job gets done.

As with any other aspect of health care, in hospice the proxy's role of advocacy can and must extend well past critical medical decision making. It is the responsibility of the proxy to see that the patient's basic care and "total pain" needs are being met completely, competently and compassionately by health care professionals.

Myth: Hospice patients must agree to die at home.

Fact: Many people believe they would prefer to die at home. Others would rather not leave that memory behind or have loved ones burdened with their 24/7 care as the end approaches. In either case, hospice care can be provided in any residential or care setting, such as a nursing home, an assisted living facility, a private residence or a hospital. Many patients begin with home-based hospice and then transfer to a care facility if their end-of-life care becomes more complex. For a residential hospice facility, room and board costs associated with a patient whose condition does not qualify for Medicare inpatient benefits may be payable by the patient.

Myth: Once admitted to hospice care, you can't get out.

Fact: If a patient's condition improves, and it is determined that he no longer qualifies because he has more than six months to live, he chooses to resume curative treatments or for any other patient-driven reason, he can leave hospice care (and return later, if he wishes to and qualifies).

Myth: Hospice is only available to those who have Medicare, private insurance with a hospice benefit or who can afford to pay for the services.

Fact: It is true that more than 9 of every 10 hospice patient days in the United States are covered by Medicare. However, if someone doesn't qualify for Medicare or Medicaid, doesn't have private health insurance and doesn't have the personal resources to pay, nonprofit hospice programs (about 30 percent of the hospice agencies nationwide) have funds available so no patient is ever turned away.[116] (Many complementary therapies and grief support not covered by Medicare are also paid for by donor funds.) Please don't be shy about asking, that's why these charitable funds exist. For-profit hospices may also have benevolent resources available to provide care services for those unable to pay.

Myth: Hospice health care providers administer pain medication to keep patients unconscious, which can make them die sooner.

Fact: The role of hospice is to make the patient as comfortable as possible for as long as possible, without the intent to either prolong dying or hasten death. Most patients' pain can be managed to allow the patient to communicate and remain alert, but some patients may suffer unbearable pain and anxiety that can only be controlled with sedation, sometimes to the point of unconsciousness. That is never done with an intent to cause or hasten death, and research has shown that the use of adequate pain medication is more likely to prolong, rather than shorten, life.

Lightbulb moment! It's a good idea to check out your community's available hospice resources, so if the need arises in the future, you'll already know your options. Anytime you hear of someone whose loved one is in hospice care or has passed away in hospice care, when the time is right, ask them about their experience. You may even have friends who currently volunteer in a hospice—that's another good source of recommendations. Call a hospice facility in your area and arrange to take a tour. Who knows? Maybe you'll decide to become a volunteer!

Chapter review

- The first modern hospice program, St. Christopher's Hospice in London, England, was started in 1967 by Dr. Cicely Saunders. She also developed the treatment protocol of addressing the patient's "total pain": the social, emotional, spiritual and physical elements of patient discomfort.

- In the United States, the first hospice was Connecticut Hospice, opened in 1974 by Florence Wald, the former dean of the Harvard School of Nursing.

- Hospice is a philosophy, an interdisciplinary approach when a cure is no longer possible or a patient chooses to discontinue curative treatment. Hospice care focuses on the dying patient's overall comfort, addressing his "total pain" with pain relief; massage; physical, speech and occupational therapies; meditation; pastoral and bereavement counseling; and complementary care such as art, aroma, music, pet, Reiki and healing touch therapies.

- With over 5,800 hospice programs in the United States, hospice is a place: wherever its patients are found. Hospice care can be provided through periodic visits by hospice professionals to a hospital, a long-term care facility (nursing home), an assisted living apartment, a private residence or an inpatient hospice facility.

- Hospice is people, serving over 1.5 million patients each year and being involved in about 43 percent of all deaths in America. Hospice professionals include physicians; nurses; hospice aides; home health care aides; social workers; speech, physical, occupational and complementary care therapists; and pastoral, bereavement and grief counselors. In addition, over 355,000 volunteers donated 16 million hours of service in 2013.

- There are many myths concerning the role of hospice care in a patient's life, what hospice benefits cover and where services are provided. It's a good idea to learn about hospice and to become familiar with your community's options for hospice care long before you or a loved one may need it.

It's most fitting to end this chapter with these words from Cicely Saunders, describing her commitment to the mission of hospice and its patients:

"You matter because you are you,
and you matter to the end of your life.
We will do all we can, not only to help you die peacefully,
but also to live until you die."

Chapter Seven
Communicating with loved ones
and health care professionals

The single biggest problem in communication
is the illusion that it has taken place.
George Bernard Shaw

The news isn't good. That's as plain as the look on Dr. Wilson's face. That cough Ernestine's been nursing for weeks (well, maybe it has been months) is more than just dry air or a bit of a cold or hay fever. He steps forward and takes Ernestine's hand in his.

Oh great, this is it, Ernestine thinks to herself. Then again, it's not like I haven't had a good life. I'm eighty-three, for heaven's sake. Let's just get this over with, doc.

"I'm afraid your tests didn't come out quite as good as I had hoped," Dr. Wilson says with an awkward half-smile. "It looks like there's something going on in your left lung. We should probably get in there and take a look-see."

Ernestine thinks before she speaks. He isn't using the Big "C"—that's a good sign. He isn't saying anything about chemo or radiation, either, like my neighbor Mabel had. That was rough. I'm not sure I'd sign up for that. Then again, if it's bad, I want to know now. I'd rather have a few weeks in my garden than months in a hospital or—heaven forbid—a nursing home.

She takes a deep breath.

"What do you think it is, doctor? Could it be cancer?"

"Oh, let's not worry about that until we have to. We'll get you scheduled for surgery and then we can talk about what's down the road. How's that sound? My nurse'll get you all set up. Good." He gives her hand a pat and leaves.

Okay, Ernestine thinks as she puts her coat on. That's not so bad. If he thought it might be cancer, he would have said that, right? Yeah, he would have said that. Okay. Good.

The Big Talk with your proxy and loved ones

Lights. Camera. Action. It's time to have The Big Talk. You've read about all the seemingly endless treatment choices if you need critical care or are at the end of life. You sort of know what you want, as much as anyone who's not currently having a major medical crisis can envision having a major medical crisis. You may not be completely sure about your directives, but even if you aren't prepared to put it all down on paper, sharing your impressions with your proxy, alternate proxy and other concerned parties is meant to be a conversation, not a speech. You may discover that talking it through, expressing your concerns out loud and listening to others' reactions or questions will help to clarify your own thinking. You may also find that you don't have a clear-cut, black letter answer for every potential situation and that's okay, too.

By now you've asked your proxy and alternate proxy to serve and they've accepted, with full understanding of their potential responsibilities. You may want to include others in The Big Talk, those likely to be nearby in a crisis, perhaps your immediate family or closest friends. That increases the odds they will one day agree that your proxy's actions are a reflection of your preferences. The proxy is the person with the legal authority, but it will make life a lot easier if everyone is on the same page, right? Without a clear understanding of the principal's preferences followed by effective written advance directives, a proxy has an unnecessary and unfair burden. Actually, two burdens: first, making blind decisions and second, justifying them to everyone else. The Big Talk will definitely minimize those burdens.

As you review and discuss these potential situations, remember it may be—actually, it is more than likely—that you will still be managing your own health care in a crisis or at life's end. The Big Talk is an opportunity to consider choices in a calm—not urgent—environment.

 Lightbulb moment! Maybe now would be the time to visit the "let's have DINNER and talk about DEATH" web site. Just sayin' . . . www.deathoverdinner.org

Health care and end-of-life scenarios

Think about the medical treatment or care you want in each of these situations, express your preferences to those gathered and then, going forward, make sure written advance directives reflect your verbal instructions.

General health care decisions

If you are temporarily incapacitated while under anesthetic, seriously ill or injured, your proxy may not need to make any decisions concerning your health care. His role may be limited to receiving updates from physicians and passing them on to family members, if that's your wish. It's advisable to review basic information on the name of your doctor and your hospital preference, if any, with your proxy and alternate proxy. Be sure they know where to find your insurance cards and policies; lists of medications, medical devices and allergies; phone numbers for any specialists you see; and a call sheet for family and friends in case of an emergency. Let them know the location of important papers, such as extra copies of your advance directives, Last Will and Testament, Durable Power of Attorney for Financial Matters (verify the identity of the person appointed in it), memorial instructions, etc.

If you suffer from a progressive disease in the future, your proxy may be the person who accompanies you on your visits to health care professionals. For some period of time, his role may simply be to stand by as your advocate without actually making any health care decisions on your behalf. But still, an invaluable presence.

Critical care and end-of-life decision making

The fictitious medical situations following here are very specific, but your responses to them will help identify the broad beliefs and values you want others to keep in mind as they face decision making on your behalf. Considering these choices for care and the use of life prolonging measures will also assist you in identifying the triggering events you want to include in your written advance directives.

As you reflect on each of these critical care medical scenarios, do so from the perspective of the future you, in the midst of these circumstances. In each scenario, ask yourself:

- What is the present goal for my medical care: to treat symptoms, to prolong life or to provide palliative care?
- Are there personal goals that I still want to reach?
- How does having or withholding the procedure further any of those goals?
- If possible, can I weigh the burdens vs. the benefits?

To make it a bit easier for you to focus on your preferences for life prolonging measures and to avoid overthinking these situations, you can approach each one with the following assumptions in mind:

- Everyone agrees you are incapacitated and unable to give informed consent, even if you are capable of some degree of communication.
- The medical condition you find yourself in has been named as a triggering event in your Living Will or combination advance directive. There is no dispute about it, the time has come to consider the use of life prolonging measures.

In weighing the benefits and burdens of using or withholding a life prolonging measure or medical treatment, keep in mind that a benefit can relieve suffering, restore a function or enhance the patient's quality of life; a burden can bring pain, prolong dying without any benefit or diminish the patient's overall quality of life.[117] As you discuss each medical scenario, share with those present the reasons for your choice, such as the religious beliefs, cultural influences or personal experiences that affect your preference. Additional insights into your general value system can be precious knowledge in the event you are someday in a medical situation that was never specifically discussed.

Decision-making scenarios

Simply put, in each situation your choices are these: 1) allow the treatment or care, 2) withhold or withdraw the treatment or care, or 3) try a time-limited trial of the treatment or care.

- You are semi-conscious and still able to acknowledge the presence of loved ones. From your body language it is obvious you are in great pain and your breathing is now labored. You can be given sufficient medication to relieve your symptoms, but that may cause you to be unconscious and totally unresponsive at the time of your death.

- You are having difficulty breathing. A ventilator will assist you, but if you cannot be weaned from it later on, which is very possible, a decision may have to be made to withdraw the ventilator, which will result in your imminent death.

- You are in the later stages of dementia, you no longer recognize your loved ones and cannot do anything for yourself, although sometimes you appear to be awake. You don't show any signs of being in pain or discomfort. You respond and safely swallow when someone prompts you repeatedly by tapping you on the chin with a spoon. The care facility is suggesting that your proxy authorize the insertion of a feeding tube or else your family needs to hire a part-time caregiver to provide assisted oral feedings for you.

- You are in a permanent vegetative state after a major stroke and are on a feeding tube. Now you've developed a respiratory infection that will probably respond to antibiotics. Treating it will likely prolong your life to some unknown extent, but if not treated, you may develop pneumonia, which will most likely cause your death.

- You have Alzheimer's disease and no longer walk or communicate, although you can safely swallow when spoon fed. Your kidneys have started to fail due to diabetes. Kidney dialysis is an option and it will most likely prolong your life.

- Your terminal disease is causing hemorrhaging that can be temporarily addressed with a blood transfusion. It will give you some relief of symptoms and will delay your death to an unknown extent.

- You suffered a stroke eight months ago, and although you appear to be conscious, you cannot speak or communicate in any way. No one can be sure if you recognize them or understand when they speak to you. You require full-time skilled nursing care, and you are now on a feeding tube because you cannot swallow without the danger of choking or aspirating (getting food into your windpipe or lungs).

- For unknown reasons, you have slipped into a coma and are unable to eat food or drink water in the usual way. The doctors do not believe you will recover from this condition. A tube can be inserted in your throat or digestive tract for food and hydration, or an intravenous line can temporarily provide nutrition.

- Your disease is incurable, your death is a matter of weeks—perhaps days—away and you are completely unresponsive. It's an exhausting burden for your loved ones to continue to care for you at home, and there is a room available at either a residential hospice facility or a local nursing home where you can receive full-time hospice and personal care. You always said you wished to die at home and you never ever wanted to go to a nursing home or any place like that.
- Although your bone cancer is beyond cure, a form of radiation will relieve some of the extreme pain you are suffering. There are possible negative side effects to the treatment, and it may also unintentionally extend your life. To treat the level of pain you are suffering, the only other alternative is sedation to unconsciousness.
- In spite of your medical condition, you are a viable organ and/or tissue donor, but you failed to sign up in your state's registry, so it's up to your loved ones to consent to or refuse donation when you die.
- You are in the final stages of dementia and your heart stops beating. Medical personnel can attempt resuscitation (CPR). Even if they are successful, you may require a ventilator on a temporary or permanent basis, or you may suffer brain damage during resuscitation. Or you might be just the same afterwards as you were when your heart stopped.
- You have been declining for some time but your condition has never been clearly diagnosed. You still know your loved ones—most days—and you now require full-time care because you cannot do anything for yourself. Your family has been taking care of you at home, which has taken a toll on them, physically, emotionally and financially. Nearby is a very nice long-term care facility where you will be safe and well cared for. Back when your health first began to decline, you made your proxy swear that he would never take you to a nursing home.
- You have a terminal condition and suddenly you're in a medical crisis. It may be an acute infection or difficulty breathing or organ failure. Your doctors have presented all the options, and your proxy has asked all the right questions. Still, the best choice just isn't obvious. Potential benefits and burdens are uncertain and no one—not even the doctors, it seems—can say what is best for you.

That last one's a toughie, isn't it? The most instructive directive you can provide may be to tell your loved ones that sometimes there is no "right" answer and that you trust them to do their best with what they know at the time. If you understand that the only option may be to focus on keeping you comfortable, share that. If you've had a great life and believe that when your time comes, you will accept and embrace your mortality, share that. If you understand that it can be frightening and confusing to know that someone you love is about to die, share that.

These are just a sampling of the possible situations that can occur at life's end. You may find more in the advance directive form you choose, which is another advantage of using one that comprehensively and clearly communicates your wishes: talking through the form together can be a sort of dress rehearsal for you and your loved ones.

> **Lightbulb moment!** If you currently have a medical condition that you think may result in unique care issues or that will require predictable end-of-life decision making, ask for your physician's input and then let your proxies and loved ones know now what they should expect and your preferences for treatment when that time comes.

Physician-patient communication

This is the story of a woman who recently had extensive—and successful—surgery for cancer. As she was recovering at home a few days later, her son casually asked if she had heard anything more about when her chemotherapy would begin. The woman could not have been more shocked. "What chemotherapy?" she demanded. Her son assured her that the surgeon had appeared as soon as she awoke in the recovery room and had explained what would happen next. The woman didn't even remember seeing her doctor—or the two days after that—never mind the content of any conversations. Did her surgeon actually believe that his patient, barely awake after a six-hour surgery, had full capacity to hear about, comprehend and consent to medical treatment? Often there's a vivid disconnect between reality and one's perception of reality, and the realm of physician-patient (or physician-proxy) communication can definitely be one of those times.

First, let's not confuse "talking" with "communicating" nor "hearing" with "comprehending." A patient or proxy who is extremely high functioning in his daily life can be rendered deaf and mute from the moment he hears the words "life-prolonging measure," and The World's Best Surgeon can also be the World's Worst Communicator. Formal studies reveal the disconnect between patients' expectations and ultimate outcomes and stories of regrets and should-have's are frequently told by survivors of patients whose lives ended without sufficient warning. These situations beg the question, Who is reality-challenged, the patients or the doctors? Not to worry, there's plenty of blame to go around. Patients and health care professionals all need to ask, What can <u>everyone</u> do to be better communicators in any phase of health care, but most especially as the end of life approaches?

The physician's role

"A physician should not be forward to make gloomy prognostications because they savour of empiricism, by magnifying the importance of his services in the treatment or cure of the disease. But he should not fail, on proper occasions, to give to the friends of

the patient timely notice of danger, when it really occurs; and even to the patient himself, if absolutely necessary. This office, however, is so peculiarly alarming when executed by him, that it ought to be declined whenever it can be assigned to any other person of sufficient judgment and delicacy. For, the physician should be the minister of hope and comfort to the sick; that, by such cordials to the drooping spirit, he may smooth the bed of death, revive expiring life, and counteract the depressing influence of those maladies which often disturb the tranquility of the most resigned, in their last moments; The life of a sick person can be shortened not only by the acts, but also by the words or the manner of a physician. It is, therefore, a sacred duty to guard himself carefully in this respect, and to avoid all things which have a tendency to discourage the patient and to depress his spirits. "[118] This advice on how to avoid being the bearer of bad tidings is from the American Medical Association's Code of Medical Ethics. The year was 1847.

The health care profession's thinking has obviously changed since then. There are now genuine experts on the subject of effective physician-patient communication who have invaluable counsel for physicians and patients alike. Dr. Atul Gawande's 2014 book *Being Mortal – Medicine and What Matters in the End* is a must-read for anyone in the medical profession or anyone who might one day use the services of the medical profession, which is pretty much everyone. Citing the work of Dr. Ezekiel Emanuel, Dr. Gawande speaks of the "interpretive model" of the physician-patient relationship, in which the doctor learns as much as possible about the patient, his lifestyle, personal goals, concerns and values and then offers treatment options to achieve goals that reflect patient priorities. You couldn't ask for a more succinct definition of the physician's initial role in shared decision making. Then together, the patient or proxy and physician consider available choices before the patient or proxy grants truly informed consent for a treatment plan.[119]

Here's another practical approach to physician-patient communication from Dr. Ferdinando L. Mirarchi. He has devised a simple checklist, an essential assessment tool for medical professionals to use in evaluating critically ill or emergency patients who may require resuscitation. The goal is to determine whether the patient's advance directives—expressed verbally or in writing—are known and incorporated into the patient's treatment plan. Called "The Resuscitation Pause" or "Advance Directive Pause," it utilizes Dr. Mirarchi's "ABCDE's of the Living Will":

A. Ask the patient or surrogate to be clear about the intentions in any existing advance directives.

B. Be clear about whether this is a Living Will triggering event or a treatable critical condition.

C. Communicate clearly whether the condition is reversible and treatable and if the prognosis is good or poor.

D. Design and discuss a plan of care with specific next steps.

E. Explain that it is okay to withhold or withdraw life sustaining treatment, and if it is the appropriate next step, explain and arrange for palliative and/or hospice care.[120]

Dr. Mirarchi's decision to include assessment of whether a triggering event has occurred is refreshingly novel. Is there any good reason to not carry his model checklist beyond the critical care or emergency arena? Using these "ABCDE's of the Living Will" seems like an obvious choice anytime a treatment plan is being crafted for a patient with an irreversible, life-limiting condition. As an outline for physician-patient communication concerning end-of-life options, it's simple and unequivocal.

The patient's role

The 1847 paternalistic model of the physician's role may, at first blush, appear so ridiculously outdated. But even in 1975, the *Quinlan* court suggested that, in the future, matters concerning the use of life prolonging measures might best be handled through ethics committees, although such deliberations "should obviously include at some stage the feelings of the family of an incompetent relative."[121] Unfortunately, as the doctor's paternalistic approach has steadily steered toward the interpretive model, it has done so without the corresponding encouragement for patients to assume the more engaged role needed to pick up the slack in the physician-patient relationship. Perhaps patients' rational for their lack of participation in health care decision making is much like their reasons for not having written advance directives: "I don't know what to do and nobody is talking to me about it." From an effective health care planning and treatment perspective, maintaining the outdated status quo is simply not in the patient's best interest. It is no longer the smart thing to do.

Here is fundamental guidance for patients in any medical setting:

- If you know ahead of time what you will be discussing with your doctor, take a list of questions with you—written down, not in your head.
- Have an "appointment buddy" present at any medical consultation; it's another set of ears and another person to pose questions.
- Be honest with your physician about your symptoms and any concerns you have.
- Do not hesitate to ask for clarification. Get over being uncomfortable saying, "I don't understand what you just said."
- Take notes, or have your appointment buddy do it. Ask for the spelling of technical or medical terms, if necessary.
- Don't leave without an understanding of the next step to be taken. And by whom.

When the time comes for treatment options to be considered and decisions to be made, fact-gathering should start with some basic questions:

- What is the diagnosis?
- Can it be cured and, if so, what are the treatment options?
- What are the potential side effects of the treatment options?
- What if there is no cure, there is a decision to stop the curative treatment or the cure doesn't work?
- What is the worst case scenario? What is the best case scenario?
- For each treatment option presented, is the goal curative, palliative or life prolonging?

For ninety percent of the physician-patient relationship, the expectation of one is to be kept well or made well by the other one. That's simple enough. So it is a fundamental shift in the physician-patient paradigm when a patient begins to understand and accept that a life-limiting condition cannot be cured. That's when the patient owes his physician clear, unambiguous communication of that acknowledgement, even if he has not quite arrived at acceptance. It's the patient's right—and as important, responsibility—to grant his physician permission to go from healing to administering comfort, from cure to care. Is it possible the patient will be the first to acknowledge the 800-pound gorilla in the room? Absolutely.

Bringing the two sides together

Doctors' communication deficiencies make them an easy target in the blame game. After all, they're the ones with all the information, right? Nevertheless, finding the way to respect a patient's goals for the remainder of his life, however long or short that may be, will only come from a physician-patient shared focus on achieving a workable strategy.

Identifying trade-offs is how Dr. Gawande approaches the challenge of customizing a patient's end of life and converting patient preferences into treatment plan action steps. In assessing a patient's goals, nothing is more personal or more individualized than understanding the specifics a person is willing to sacrifice in order to have the "best possible day, however they might define it under the circumstances."[122] Likewise, when it comes to effective communication, it seems that physicians, patients and proxies should all be practicing Dr. Mirarchi's "Advance Directive Pause" so that health care professionals get the critical information they need, maybe even before they ask for it. How better to merge patients' care preferences with the reality of a medical crisis than to have everyone reading from the same script?

A common belief is that a "good death" centers on how the patient defines "quality of life." But even "quality of life" implies a comparative value across a population. Remember, no groupthink allowed here. A terminal or irreversible life-limiting condition warrants a goal-oriented treatment plan that grants absolute deference to the patient's unique perspective. To achieve that, there's certain information the physician needs from the patient, but first the patient has to ask himself some challenging questions. What parts of life—given the available alternatives—does he most wish to preserve? What are his greatest concerns? What makes him anxious or afraid? Is independence his touchstone? The ability to communicate with loved ones? To feed himself? To have enough time to say goodbye? To write a letter to family and friends? To have a party? To seek forgiveness or to say "I love you"? To share that favorite family recipe one more time? To achieve at least a few goals on his Bucket List? To know when death is close?

The questions that only the patient can answer.

By definition, "communication" is an exchange of information. It requires a solid, two-way dialogue in order to build a physician-patient relationship that is meaningful as well as functional.

The health care proxy's unique perspective

Meanwhile, the health care proxy is rolled up in a ball in the corner of the room, having his own issues. Whether appointed by the principal or serving as a default surrogate decision maker recognized by law, his duty is to evaluate options, make choices based on the patient's advance directives—if known—and give informed consent to the health care professionals' recommended treatment plan. As such, he's entitled to the same information the patient would be entitled to, but the proxy has dual roles as both a rational decision maker and, quite probably, a grieving family member or close friend facing the imminent loss of a loved one, the patient.

Lightbulb moment! As patient or proxy, if you have some forewarning that a conversation with a health care professional is going to involve decision making, don't hesitate to take your checklist of questions along. If you're caught unawares and you can't seem to pull your thoughts together, let the doctor know that. If time for decision making allows, ask to reconvene when you have someone with you, or ask if you can schedule a time to meet again very soon to cover the questions you know you'll have but you just haven't yet thought of.

The proxy often serves as the primary source of information for other loved ones. He's the voice of reason, the peacemaker and, sometimes, the messenger that everyone wants to shoot. As witness to the patient's decline toward death, the proxy deserves to ask the questions that are unique to him and that merit answers from health care professionals:

- Have we discussed all the most likely outcomes and what's to be expected?
- Are we doing everything we can to provide compassionate palliative care?

- What do these hospital or hospice status "codes" mean? How do they translate into the level or type of care the patient will receive?
- Will we know when the patient is about to die? Is it safe to leave the patient's side for a while?
- What will death look like? What will we observe when it is near?
- Can the patient still hear me and does he know I am present?
- What happens after the patient dies?
- Is it all right for us to stay with the body and to have religious rites at the bedside?
- Am I doing my job as the health care proxy and am I doing it well?

The best advance directives on the planet aren't of much use if you don't recognize when the time has come to refer to them. Patients and proxies deserve clear communication of the vital information they need to make meaningful and timely end-of-life plans. Health care professionals deserve permission to accept and acknowledge that not treating the patient's condition is not the same as not treating the patient.

Chapter review

- In preparing to execute written advance directives, once you're familiar with your potential choices for care if you're in a critical or end-of-life medical situation, it's time to communicate your preferences to your proxy and loved ones.
- For The Big Talk, you should include those who have agreed to serve as proxy and alternate proxy and any others likely to be nearby in a future crisis, probably your immediate family or closest friends.
- It is advisable to review with your proxies basic information on the names of your health care professionals, your preference of hospital and where to find information on your regular medications, allergies and medical devices.
- The role of the proxy may initially be to simply accompany the principal to health care appointments, acting as an engaged, albeit silent, advocate.
- As you discuss potential critical medical scenarios, talk about the reasons for your choice in each case. That will give your proxies and loved ones additional insight into your general belief and value system.
- Patients and health care professionals all need to ask what they can do to be better communicators.
- As outlined by Dr. Atul Gawande, in shared decision making the doctor learns as much as possible about the patient, his lifestyle, personal goals, concerns and values and then offers treatment options to achieve those goals and to reflect patient priorities. Together, the patient or proxy and physician consider choices before the patient or proxy ultimately grants truly informed consent.

- A checklist such as Dr. Ferdinando L. Mirarchi's "The Advance Directive Pause" utilizes an assessment approach to coordinating a patient's advance directives with his treatment plan. It is also a valuable tool for patients, proxies and physicians to focus their evaluative thinking on the goals of treatment in any medical situation.

- Once he has the information he needs for decision making and understands the terminal nature of his condition, it's the patient's right—and as important, responsibility—to grant his physician permission to go from healing to administering comfort, from cure to care.

- By definition, "communication" is an exchange of information. It requires a solid, two-way dialogue to build a physician-patient relationship that is meaningful as well as functional.

- As witness to the patient's decline toward imminent death, the proxy is entitled to the same information the patient would be entitled to, but the proxy has dual roles as both a rational decision maker and, quite probably, a grieving family member or close friend facing the imminent loss of a loved one, the patient.

Chapter Eight
The "what ifs" of advance directives

No more prizes for predicting rain.
Prizes only for building arks.
Anonymous

Every fall, just like clockwork, Chester and Irene load up the car and head for snowbird country. They've rented the same park model double-wide for the past 15 years. It's a relief to get out of the Midwest before the winter weather comes, and sometimes their daughter and her family fly in and join them for spring break. With all of Chester's health issues, after Irene attends that adult education class about advance directives, she insists they talk about their wishes for care if they ever get into a jam. They both agree that eating through a tube is no life at all, and they make sure daughter Chrissie knows what she's to do if anything like that is about to happen.

Chester tells Chrissie that if he can't get himself down to the coffee shop each morning, life is not worth living. Irene says if she can't play the piano for the grandkids, there's no use hanging around. Chrissie smiles and says she understands. Chester and Irene have every intention of getting it all written down in a proper manner, but before you know it, October rolls around and they need to hit the road if they're going to stay ahead of the season's first snowstorm. Irene makes a mental note to ask their winter friends to recommend an attorney once they get settled in the double-wide.

Chester has his heart attack just outside Tulsa, Oklahoma. They manage to keep him alive in the emergency room but he just doesn't wake up. Chrissie arrives and after a few days, she stands by as her mother tells the attending physician that Chester doesn't want a feeding tube, and they've all accepted that it's his time to go.

The doctor shakes his head. "Here in Oklahoma, we use CPR and feeding tubes unless somebody can show us that the patient doesn't want that. Since I just met your husband, I can't say I know he isn't in-it-to-win-it. The good news is, your husband's condition isn't terminal, so rest assured, we'll be doing everything possible to sustain his life until he has another heart attack, and we're not able to bring him back around."

That's certainly not what Chester and Irene wanted, now is it? Maybe it's possible to avoid a calamity like they're experiencing by being aware of what can happen if the simple four-step plan isn't followed from beginning to end. It's time to put some of the knowledge you've gathered to the test and talk about the "what-ifs" of advance health care planning.

What if there are no written advance directives?

Only about 28 percent of all American adults have put their advance directives into writing. Reality has a way of turning a paradigm on its head, so here's hoping that participation rate improves over time. Meanwhile, the good news is that about two thirds of all adults have either talked about or written down their thoughts on end-of-life treatment. That means that even if they haven't gotten around to putting them into writing, about 40 percent have at least voiced their opinions (and the chances of that happening increase dramatically with age).[123] In the absence of a Living Will and Durable Power of Attorney for Health Care, any previously expressed verbal preferences are useful input for the physician and the patient's proxy-by-statute.

The *Cruzan* court offers solid guidance to the physician and the proxy-by-statute in proceeding as the patient would want them to. Any previous clear-cut verbal directives get first priority. Then, for the third of American adults who have neither talked about nor written down their wishes,[124] the physician and the proxy-by-statute consider what the patient would do, based on general or specific evidence of his beliefs, values and attitudes about life; that's the definition of "substituted judgment." Hopefully, someone who truly knows the patient can enlighten the attending physician on specifics. If there's no clue as to what the patient would want, the attending physician and proxy-by-statute should jointly decide what is in the patient's best interest. Having said all that, remember that in some states, certain medical procedures are not allowed without clear and convincing evidence of the patient's intent.

What if there's a Durable Power of Attorney for Health Care and no Living Will?

Some people might say, who needs a Living Will if you've appointed an awesome proxy in a Durable Power of Attorney for Health Care? And that may be true if your proxy knows you and knows what you want and is willing and able to make the tough calls.

However, even having had The Big Talk, without the written evidence of a Living Will, it can be argued that the patient's wishes are not being honored by the proxy. That's when the absence of a Living Will equates to the absence of clear and convincing evidence of the patient's intent. *Quinlan* and *Cruzan* demonstrated the potential for a dispute when the patient's wishes are either unknown or unclear. It is virtually impossible to validate a patient's verbal wishes to the satisfaction of a physician (or outside party) who is reluctant to agree with the proxy's instructions and doesn't want to be convinced otherwise. Again, any state law "clear and convincing" standard may or may not be met in the absence of express written instructions from the patient in the form of a Living Will.

What if there's a Living Will
and no Durable Power of Attorney for Health Care?

If a patient has written care instructions (a Living Will) but has not appointed a proxy in writing, the patient's attending physician should be guided by the contents of the Living Will. State law may require the joint agreement of an attending physician and a recognized proxy-by-statute in order for life prolonging decisions to be withheld or withdrawn. That requires that someone on the statutory list is willing and able to act as the stand-in proxy.

Having no qualified prospect available to be appointed as proxy could be due to a shortage of those possessing the decision-making capability to act for another. Spouse already has dementia? No adult children? All the close friends are also elderly and frail? In lieu of appointing a qualified proxy, having a detailed, comprehensive Living Will is crucial. It's also important for the declarant to discuss the contents of the Living Will with the primary doctor and even the personal attorney ahead of time. Then the patient will have the benefit of advocates who know him and can validate the terms of his Living Will, even if no one is cast in the official role of a proxy (a personal physician is restricted from serving as his patient's proxy, legally and ethically speaking, but a personal attorney may be an appropriate choice).

Depending on the specifics of the situation, it may be prudent to establish a standby guardianship in the event of future incapacity for someone who does not have a suitable candidate in the statutory line of default surrogate decision makers.

> **Lightbulb moment!** If you don't already have a Durable Power of Attorney for Health Care, stop and think whether you would be comfortable having one or more of those who qualify under your state's proxy-by-statute law as your default surrogate decision maker(s). Is he or she available, capable, trustworthy, able to ask the tough questions, familiar with your preferences? If not, put this process of choosing, communicating with and appointing a proxy and alternate proxy on the fast track, or pursue other available alternatives, such as a standby guardianship.

What if an advance directive is defective under state law?

In theory, state advance directive statutes provide uniformity in order to foster clarity and reduce questions of intent or legitimacy. Formalities such as witness requirements or even mandated language exist to keep everyone playing by the same rules. So, how serious is an infraction of those rules? For example, what if a Living Will is perfectly valid in all respects except state law requires two witnesses and only one appears on the document? In all likelihood, it's a nonissue. That's because the law gives deference to any specific written or oral care instructions expressed by the patient, even in the absence of every crossed "t" and dotted "i." If there are <u>no</u>

witnesses and the patient's capacity when the document was signed is later in doubt, the missing witnesses will be an issue because of the inability to verify competence, not because it's a violation of the state's execution requirements.

To be very clear, this discussion is about technical form and/or execution issues, not whether the directive adequately addresses the medical situation at hand. For instance, if dementia is named as a triggering event with an instruction to forego "feeding provided artificially," then don't expect health care providers—or a court of law—to honor a proxy's instructions to stop spoon feeding the patient, even if he claims that's what the patient meant to say. That is a question of ineffective drafting, not an issue of being a defective advance directive under state law formality requirements.

It's not that formal documentation requirements are not important—at times, even crucial—but the invalidity of a written advance directive as to format only becomes an issue if there is conflict over what care should be provided. Otherwise, the legal system leans toward giving all possible deference to the wishes of the patient, in spite of technical faults.

What if you're travelling away from home?

Attempting to draft an advance directive form that will satisfy all existing states' requirements "would create a paper monster, looking something like an elephant with an ostrich's head, tiger fangs, bunny feet, fish fins, and wings."[125] Yipes. There's a legal concept known as "comity" (not to be confused with comedy), which is much like "reciprocity," in which state governments say to each other: "We'll honor yours if you'll honor ours." When it comes to written advance directives, most states accept the validity of properly executed forms from another state. By now you're not surprised to learn there are exceptions, are you? Some states only accept others' Durable Powers of Attorney for Health Care, some only accept Living Wills and some don't accept either one.[126] It does add an element of suspense when you travel across state lines. And what of visits to another country?

When it comes to foreign travel, believe it or not, there are places on Earth where they don't even know what an advance directive is, and you should absolutely not assume that the culture or health care system of another country recognizes yours. Add the legal effect of advance directives to your list of pre-trip research, right after health insurance coverage and available medical care.

As for travel within the United States, just look what happened to poor Chester. When he and his wife Irene decided to spin the wheel of life and hit the road without written advance directives, they should have taken a big detour around Oklahoma. Contrary to what many state laws and advance directive forms presume (that a person does not want life prolonging measures), Oklahoma takes the opposite view. Unless otherwise shown, incapacitated persons are presumed to want CPR and artificial nutrition and hydration. There are ways around that but Chester's situation doesn't qualify. Oh, by the way, Oklahoma would have had no problem accepting Chester's out-of-state Living Will as long as it had contained specific language about artificial nutrition and hydration. Or, if Chester had appointed Irene as his proxy in a Durable Power of Attorney for Health Care, she could request a Do Not Resuscitate order on his behalf. As it is, she'll have to go to court and present evidence that Chester didn't want a feeding tube. With 20/20 hindsight, Chester and Irene might decide that hittin' the road without written advance directives wasn't the prudent thing to do.

Not to pick on Oklahoma, but its law is such a model example of the importance of having written advance directives, it was difficult to pass up.[127] It's also a sobering illustration of the havoc that the diversity among states' advance directive laws can wreak. The best anyone can do is to prepare written advance directives in compliance with the state of residence and consider the law of any other regularly visited states. Also take into account proxy availability if you're 1,500 miles away at your winter home when a crisis occurs. Do-it-yourself advance directive forms aren't bad in and of themselves—mostly because they make the process accessible and affordable—but this is an example of when it makes sense to have an attorney review your efforts to ensure you have anticipated and addressed interstate compliance issues as much as possible.

Chapter review

- If there are no written advance directives, the patient's verbal instructions are first considered, then his general or specific values, views and attitudes about life.
- When a proxy has been appointed but there is no Living Will—no written care instructions—the health care providers and proxy should follow the patient's verbal instructions, if any.
- For the patient who has written care directives but does not have a Durable Power of Attorney for Health Care—no health care proxy has been appointed—health care professionals should be guided by the Living Will instructions. If necessary, a proxy-by-statute may be recognized.
- Even if a written advance directive is defectively formatted or executed according to state law, the patient's written instructions will probably be honored unless there is a conflict among caregivers or family members.
- For travel outside the state of residence, one should verify the compliance of a written advance directive with any other state's form or content requirements. When travelling outside the country, assume nothing.

Chapter Nine
Putting it all together with written advance directives

How wonderful it is that nobody need wait a single moment
before starting to improve the world.
Anne Frank

"What can I say?" Dottie always says. "I'm an over-achiever." Yup, she has an up-to-date Last Will and Testament, a detailed household inventory, neatly labeled folders for her medical records, the deed to the house, the title to the car, etc. Her written advance directives, thoughtfully prepared, are fully communicated to her proxy and alternate proxy and are now handy in the top drawer of her living room desk—a wallet card is in her billfold, of course.

Everyone thinks she's a bit over the top on this. You know, she's very healthy for a seventy-five year old, certainly compared to most of her friends. Why so obsessive about preparing for the end of life, they always ask, shaking their heads. And Dottie always answers, "You know me, I like everything neat and tidy."

Nobody expects that city bus to hit her, least of all Dottie. If she'd been able to speak afterwards, she would have just shrugged and said, "It was all my fault—I was too busy looking at the pretty holiday lights to notice that silly bus making a left hand turn, right into my crosswalk. Can you imagine? Oh, and don't forget to pick up everyone's presents—they're already wrapped and under the tree."

Instead, she's in intensive care, she isn't saying anything and it isn't looking too good for Dottie. The doctor explains to Dottie's best friend and proxy, Louise, that besides the broken pelvis and leg, Dottie has a back injury they won't really be able to judge unless she wakes up and—here's the thing—that's probably not going to happen. She's taken a bad hit to the head and the MRI isn't conclusive but, well, now there's brain swelling. Dottie's starting to have trouble breathing; they need to consider whether to put her on a ventilator.

Louise pulls herself together and looks over Dottie's Living Will one more time. That's just a nervous reaction because she already knows what it says. She knew before today and she's read it another ten times while sitting in the waiting room.

"The truth is, doctor, her Living Will says we can put her on a ventilator, but only if it's for a short time while she gets better. What do you think?"

He says he doesn't know for sure if she'll need the ventilator permanently, but he doesn't think the chances of her getting better are very good. But they'll try it if that's what Louise thinks is best.

Louise goes on. "And there's something else, something not here in the paperwork, doctor. Dottie told me about a zillion times that she would rather say her adieus than ever have to live in a nursing home. She's very independent and social and she couldn't imagine giving up all that. She'll be spending a lot of time in a nursing home if she does wake up, right?"

The doctor nods. No question about that. There would be months of rehabilitation, at best. But he doesn't want to mislead Louise, he says, because he's as sure as any human can be that Dottie will not be waking up.

Louise signs the authorization to withhold the ventilator. She stays at Dottie's side, holding her hand for the two hours until she peacefully passes. It's what Louise would want Dottie to do for her if the tables were turned—and she knows Dottie would.

It can happen. It's not often enough that the patient prepares the right paperwork, chooses the right proxy and says all the right things, but it can happen. There's a whole lot about the circumstances leading to life's end that's unpredictable, but documentation and communication are two things you can control.

The finish line is approaching, the end of this journey toward understanding choices and creating meaningful and effective health care advance directives. You've been soaking up an incredible amount of information about the medical and legal implications of care and treatment options. Just to clarify, none of the following qualify as advance directives:

- "I trust you—you'll know what to do."
- "Just pull the plug!"
- "I don't want to be a vegetable."
- "Sorry, but I can't talk about this—it's too sad for me."
- "When the time comes, just let me go."

Not one of them clearly communicates the patient's preferences for care at life's end. Sadly, that can also be said for many of the advance directive forms floating around these days. This is the heart of the **documentation** step of the simple four-step process. This chapter covers the minimal requirements for effective written advance directives, where to find forms that best fit your needs and what to do with them once they're fully executed.

The purpose of written advance directives is to give enforceability to intent, because it's much easier to understand and carry out a person's instructions if they are clearly expressed in black and white. Written advance directives have been around for about forty years. While life prolonging and life extending medical treatments have progressed by leaps and bounds, the legal documentation complementing that evolution has been in the snail mode, and its shortcomings have become all too obvious. Thanks to those who have watched and learned, along with the easy access offered by the Internet, it's a new day and a new way, and there are now a variety of worthy options to choose from.

Important to know: In eight states (Alabama, Indiana, Kansas, New Hampshire, Ohio, Oregon, Texas and Utah), the use of the advance directive form contained within the state code is required.[128] To avoid unintentional conflicts or confusion about what you meant to say—which can lead to unenforceable provisions—you should not attach other documents or language to any of these state forms without the counsel of a competent estate, elder law or family law attorney.

Minimum standards –
The Durable Power of Attorney for Health Care

An effective Durable Power of Attorney for Health Care has to contain certain elements to qualify as complete and legally enforceable. Forms provided by recognized organizations usually comply, but check any form you are considering against this list anyway. At a minimum, a Durable Power of Attorney for Health Care should include:

- The event that triggers the proxy's powers, usually the principal's general lack of decision-making capacity. It may specify the method of confirmation, by either referencing or mimicking state law requirements.
- The appointment of a proxy to act on behalf of the principal and to make decisions concerning the principal's health care.
- The appointment of at least one alternate proxy (not a co-proxy) in the event the first named proxy is not available or is unable or unwilling to serve.
- The health care decision-making powers granted to the proxy by the principal, including access to medical records.
- Any limitations on powers granted to the proxy.
- Execution, witnessing and notarization as required by the laws of the state of the principal's residence. (Restrictions on who can serve as witnesses for a written advance directive are common in state laws.)

Minimum standards – The Living Will

An effective Living Will must contain certain elements to qualify as complete and legally enforceable. Forms provided by recognized organizations usually comply, but check any form you are considering against this list anyway. At a minimum, a Living Will should include:

- One or more events that trigger the terms of the Living Will. To be truly useful to the physician and proxy, triggering events should describe the declarant/patient's condition or his degree of interaction with his environment, rather than specify a narrow medical diagnosis.
- Whether and when life sustaining measures should be given or withheld, with specific reference to the principal's choices regarding artificial nutrition and hydration (tubal feeding), mechanical ventilation (a ventilator) and kidney

dialysis. The declarant may also consider the inclusion of guidelines for the use of assisted oral feeding (spoon feeding). Caution: check your state's law to make sure you have satisfied any requirements for express consent to certain medical procedures.

- Whether and when medical treatments such as antibiotics, blood transfusions, hospitalization, surgery, radiation and chemotherapy should be given or withheld.
- Whether and when a written Do Not Resuscitate order (DNR) should be obtained.
- Whether and when medical devices should be removed or deactivated.
- Preferences as to the use of palliative care such as pain management and alternative therapies meant to provide comfort.
- If there is a preference and if a choice is available, where the declarant/patient prefers to die, whether hospice care is desired as the end of life approaches and specifics as to any religious rituals and environmental comforts.
- Whether the declarant/patient wishes to be an organ, eye and tissue donor, if possible. (Registration in the state's donor registry is also recommended.)
- Execution, witnessing and notarization as required by the laws of the state of residence. (Restrictions on who can serve as witnesses for a written advance directive are common in state laws.)

Lightbulb moment! A note about having your signature witnessed. The following people should not serve as witnesses for the execution of your advance directive: the proxy or alternate proxy, your physician or people employed by any care facility where you reside, a person responsible to pay for your health care, an employee of your life or health insurance carrier, a member of your family and anyone who might be a creditor of your estate.[129]

The combination advance directive form

An alternative to having the two traditional advance directive documents (a Durable Power of Attorney for Health Care and a Living Will) is to have one document that performs both functions. It contains the appointment of a health care proxy, and it details the care instructions to be carried out by the patient's health care professionals and proxy. (Please remember what was said in Chapter Two: In a combination advance directive, the portion of the document in which a proxy is appointed is the same as a Durable Power of Attorney for Health Care, and the portion of the document in which life prolonging measures are addressed is the same as a Living Will.) Besides the convenience of requiring only one set of signatures, there are other distinct advantages to using a well-drafted combination advance directive:

- Lack of availability is a common criticism of written advance directives in general; having a combination form reduces by one the number of documents to keep track of.
- You want your proxy to be the advocate for your care instructions, so it makes sense to have the proxy's appointment in close proximity to the proxy's instructions, all in one document.
- Having only one form ensures there are no unintentional conflicts created between separate advance directive documents.
- Unless you have a valid reason for only appointing a proxy or only recording your care instructions, executing a combination directive ensures that both steps are taken, simultaneously (and you always reserve the right to strike out and initial any part of a combination form that does not apply to your situation).
- Using a combination form encourages the inclusion of preferences concerning other end-of-life issues, such as organ donation, comfort care and disposition of the declarant's body. Those are important instructions that don't really fit in either a traditional Living Will or a Durable Power of Attorney for Health Care. The inconvenience of inclusion usually means those issues are not addressed.
- Last, but most important, there's all that potential confusion over the issue of whether a triggering event has occurred. "Is this one?" "Should I be looking at the Living Will now?" "Does this medical condition qualify?" Having a combination advance directive form reinforces the practical reality that the health care proxy is in the role of health care decision maker <u>anytime</u> the principal cannot be, which reduces the either/or implications of a traditional Living Will.

> **Lightbulb moment!** Visit your state's site for elder care or your state medical association or bar association sites to sample additional forms. I'm not saying they're more or less likely to be well-drafted or appropriate forms—but you won't know until you look.

The cost of preparing advance directives

Like many things in life, you can spend as much or as little as you want when it comes to preparing advance directive forms. If you do have an attorney assist in the preparation of your written advance directives—which is highly recommended—the cost will be minimal if you do your homework before you arrive at the attorney's office. An estimate—just an estimate, mind you—is that it will cost $150-300 to have advance directive documents prepared for two people. That assumes the attorney already has a good form on hand (if he doesn't, you're using the wrong attorney). You can ask ahead of time for an estimate, you know—and you should if cost is a concern to you. For lawyers, time is money, and if you choose to spend yours—time and money, that is—sitting in front of the attorney kicking around the idea of which child would make the best proxy or how you really feel about the whole idea of cremation, please do so. But expect to pay for the use of his or her office while you ponder the parts of the process that only you can tackle. To save time and money complete the list of **Review and to do** tasks at the end of this chapter before your visit.

If you prefer, ask your attorney to email or mail to you the directive form he favors before your appointment so you can preview it at your leisure. If you're not sure it covers all you want it to, go ahead and sample other available forms. The attorney's job is to make sure your advance directives are clearly documented in compliance with your state's law and in keeping with your wishes as you have expressed them to him or her. Many attorneys automatically draft advance directives when asked to prepare a Last Will and Testament (another document that can be done at a minimal cost if your strategizing is done outside the lawyer's office). This would be an opportune time to review all the legal documents mentioned in Chapter Three. And there's something to be said for retaining the services of a person who comes fully equipped with witnesses, a notary public and a copy machine.

Preparing written advance directives can indeed be a do-it-yourself project, and assuming you use a good form, in most cases you'll be just fine. If you decide to go the DIY route, you'll find that many advance directive forms are available for free or at very low cost. Here's another thought: how about organizing a group of folks who all want to get advance directives off their To Do list and tackle it together? And how about asking a local elder law attorney to facilitate the gathering? See **For further information** for group presentation resources.

Lightbulb moment! Make the most of your time when you visit your attorney. Verify the spelling of names and contact information for your proxy and alternate proxy before you go. If you're updating other legal documents (see Chapter Three), have names, contact info, dates of birth and Social Security numbers for all executors, beneficiaries and heirs. Verify how title is currently held to assets such as real estate, bank and retirement accounts, vehicles, etc. If your current legal documents were not prepared by the attorney you're now using, take them along as well.

Where to get an advance directive form

Some states have their own opinion of the ideal advance directive form. If you are a resident of a state (Alabama, Indiana, Kansas, New Hampshire, Ohio, Oregon, Texas and Utah) that mandates the use of a statutory directive, please discuss its effectiveness with an attorney. In some other states, statutory forms or language are provided (read: suggested) but not required.

As for state-mandated and state-suggested forms in general: just because legalese has undergone the rigorous review of a bunch of legislators most certainly does not imply it is the best form, or the best form for you. It's worth repeating that when a document presupposes what a person wants, it is known as a "default option" or "default response" form, and for written advance directives, the default option is for no life prolonging measures, period. Unless its terms coincide exactly with a particular declarant's intent, a default option Living Will is a bad form. Most people either 1) don't really understand its meaning, 2) don't know how to amend the form to reflect their own preferences if they do understand it or 3) don't feel comfortable doing so. As a result, a default option form tends to strongly influence the declarant's decision to execute it as-is, whether or not it reflects the declarant's preferences.[130] If it doesn't, the form is not doing its job and that makes it a bad form.

In searching for an advance directive form that does what you want it to do, lean toward those of the multiple choice variety. Some present two or three options for each type of life prolonging procedure or may even contain potential medical scenarios with accompanying choices. Many also provide the opportunity to add any special circumstances or instructions not already addressed in the form (with the help of legal counsel, please).

Lightbulb moment! IMPORTANT CAUTIONARY NOTE: If you want to embellish any advance directive form, do so only with the assistance of competent legal counsel. There's amending and there's addending (I made that up) and then there's just plain making a mess. It takes a trained legal wordsmith to avoid creating conflicting or confusing provisions within or between documents and to verify that applicable law does not invalidate any provision of your altered advance directives.

The advance directive form recommended in the first edition of this book was *Five Wishes®*, distributed by the nonprofit organization Aging with Dignity. Nine years later, it still is. For the money (it's $5 for a single copy and $1 if you get 24 friends to join you), it's a bargain of a form and a combination advance directive that includes all the necessary elements:

- The appointment of a substitute decision maker;
- The medical care and life prolonging measures you want;
- The comfort care you want;
- How you want to be treated by the people around you; and
- Any message you want to leave with your loved ones (a mini Ethical Will).

As a bonus, *Five Wishes®* is accepted in 42 states and the District of Columbia (think: what Irene and Chester should have had). The Aging With Dignity web site also provides any state-specific requirements, such as witnessing. *Five Wishes®* can be attached to any of the eight state-mandated forms, but if you choose to do that, please see an attorney for assistance. Without that legal counsel, you may create irresolvable conflicts between the two documents. (For the record, Five Wishes® is recommended here solely because it's inexpensive, straightforward and does the job. Oh, and it makes a great outline for The Big Talk with your proxies and other stakeholders.)

There are many advance directive forms available, usually provided by nonprofit organizations, and one might be a better choice for your unique needs. There are also countless excellent forms developed by attorneys for the use of their own clients. Share what you have learned with your lawyer. Coupled with his or her legal expertise, the two of you should be able to craft the ideal written advance directive—just for you! To be honest, you may have to kiss a few frogs before you find the princely form you're meant to use.

Lightbulb moment! You don't go to a podiatrist if you're having problems with your eyes. If you want to get competent legal counsel on end-of-life issues, see an attorney who specializes in estate, elder or family law. The best route is to ask your friends for names of lawyers who know what they're doing, or seek a referral from a trusted attorney who happens to practice in another area of law. If the advance directive form provided in your state's code is bad, you want an attorney who has found—or created—a better one. They're out there, just keep looking.

The effect of HIPAA on advance directives

If you've visited any type of health care provider in the past nine years, you've signed a HIPAA (Health Insurance Portability and Accountability Act of 1996) Notice and Privacy Form. By your signature you designated who, if anyone, can see your medical records. Without that authorization HIPAA severely limits access. The question relevant to our discussion is whether this federal law in any way affects the validity of a Durable Power of Attorney for Health Care or the powers of a health care proxy.

The simple answer is "probably not." There are assurances on the official government HIPAA site stating that "Nothing in the Privacy Rule changes the way in which an individual grants another person power of attorney for health care decisions. State law (or other law) regarding health care power of attorney continues to apply."[131] It has been suggested by some sources that because the proxy's power (read: to do and see whatever the principal can do and see) doesn't kick in until the principal lacks decision-making capacity, under HIPAA, the proxy won't be able to access the principal's medical records until that determination has been made. That was always the case; a proxy doesn't achieve decision-making power, including access to medical records, until the principal lacks decision-making power.

If you or your legal counsel is concerned about this, you can add authorizing language in your Durable Power of Attorney for Health Care stating that the authorization to view medical records—solely—is effective upon execution of the

Durable Power of Attorney for Health Care; the triggering event of incapacity will not need to first occur. Or the principal can sign a separate HIPAA Notice and Privacy Form, granting medical record access to the proxy and alternative proxy. If the proxy named in the Durable Power of Attorney for Health Care is the one who accompanies the principal to doctors' appointments, he may already be designated in the provider's records.

Review and to do

Now you're ready to choose and execute advance directives that reflect your choices about medical and end-of-life care. Whether tackling this on your own or with the assistance of legal counsel—which is highly recommended—first taking the following steps will smooth the way:

- Become familiar with the advance directive laws of your state and any other state's law to which you may be subject. If needed, seek competent legal counsel to get a thorough understanding of your state's law and any requirements that may directly affect the content of your written advance directives.

- If you previously executed advance directives, review them for compliance with current law and your current wishes for medical care. If your written advance directives are now inapplicable for any reason—if the proxy appointment is no longer suitable or the instructions are incomplete—plan to prepare and execute new ones.

- Considering the law and your personal preferences, learn what type of advance directive form is accepted in your state and will most effectively reflect your wishes and instructions.

- Think about creating your Ethical Will as a first step before crafting your written advance directives (see the next chapter for more information on that).

- Narrow your choices for a proxy and alternate proxy, using the criteria in Chapter Four. Focus on those who are available, willing and able to be your health care advocate if you become incapacitated. Choose a proxy and an alternate proxy, ask each one to serve, explaining what their duties as proxy may include. If you get a "no," ask someone else.

- Have The Big Talk with your proxies and loved ones using an advance directive form and/or Chapter Seven of this book as your guide to discussing potential medical scenarios. While sharing your preferences, include your values and general beliefs about what living an independent, fulfilling life means to you. If possible, include anyone who may be present in a medical crisis. Express your trust in your proxies to do what is in your best interest if a situation arises that you have not discussed.

- Select an advance directive form from an independent source or visit with your attorney to get one. You may even want to share one you like with your attorney.

He or she can advise you on incorporating language into a form they recommend or assist you with completing and executing the form you have chosen as the best one for you.

> **Lightbulb moment!** Even if your state's law does not require it, use at least two witnesses, and have your signature and your witnesses' signatures notarized. Then you've met the requirements of all states. And fully execute your written advance directives (signed, witnessed and notarized) as soon as they are available. If prepared by your attorney, tell him or her to call when the written advance directives are ready. Read them thoroughly before signing, then have your signature witnessed and notarized before you leave the attorney's office. Have at least 10 copies made.

Caring for advance directives

Advance directives are of no value unless they are accessible to health care providers and the proxy. The final step in the **communication** process is to make sure that everyone who needs access to your written health care advance directives has access. Don't stop now.

Distributing copies of written advance directives

Once your written advance directives are properly signed, witnessed and notarized, it's time to distribute them to others and carefully store the originals and your copies.

- Your estate attorney (the attorney most familiar with your legal matters) should have a copy even if he or she did not prepare or provide the written advance directives you are using.
- Give a copy to your proxy and to your alternate proxy. Review the documents with them to make sure everyone—including you—understands what they say.
- Give a copy to any other family member, friend or caregiver likely to accompany you to any future medical procedure or emergency hospital trip.
- If you choose to, on your next visit, give a copy to your primary physician and to any other specialists you visit on a regular basis. Take a few minutes to make sure each one is aware of the contents, and express your feelings about end-of-life care. You may choose to register your form online with your health care provider, if that is an available option.
- Keep two or three additional copies at home so you can take one along if you are hospitalized, have an out-patient procedure or go to a care or rehabilitation facility.
- You keep the original in a safe place (about that in a moment).

- Carry a card in your wallet (right behind your driver's license—that's the first place emergency personnel will look). It should show that you have written advance directives and have the names and contact information for your proxy, alternate proxy and your primary physician. If, for a valid reason, your emergency contact is someone other than your proxy or alternate proxy, show that contact info first. Indicate organ donor registration on your driver's license or photo ID as well.

- Consider writing an Ethical Will for your loved ones to leave a record of what you stand for and how you would like to be remembered (see Chapter Ten).

- Remember to make arrangements for the care of Fido and Fluffy by discussing your wishes for their care with your—sorry, their—veterinarian on the next visit.

Lightbulb moment! If you've designated an "emergency contact" person with your physician, etc., is it the same person as your proxy? If not, shouldn't it be? You'd be surprised how often that is not the case. Think about it: if you are in a medical emergency, the doctors will turn for guidance to the person who's present, not the person named in a document in the possession of the person who's not present.

Storing written advance directives

A word about storing the originals of any valuable documents. Yes, they should be safe and protected, but a safety deposit box is the place for documents that you do not need in an emergency. It may not be opened for some time after your death, long past when your written advance directives will be of use. Without naming names, some people might suggest keeping important papers in a canister in the freezer, in the theory that it would be the very last item to float away or burn up. This may be good advice, but maybe not. Sorry, Mom.

Actually, where you keep your written advance directives is not as critical as who knows where that is. Whether it's in your desk, in a fire-retardant box, in the kitchen junk drawer or on the closet shelf in a clearly marked container, the primary person who will look after you if you get sick or injured probably already knows where your important papers are, right? Really, they don't? Well, then now would be a good time to tell them. Also, it's important that your loved ones be able to find copies of your advance directives if they cannot locate their own copies in an emergency. Be sure originals are accessible and protected from fire and water in a security bag or box.

As for your own extra copies, you can keep one in the glove compartment of your car, your purse or in an envelope with bold printing on the front near your car keys. No matter where they are kept, the important thing is that you and significant others know where to find them. The other reason to put your written advance directives where they are easily accessible is to act as a friendly reminder that you need to occasionally review and possibly revise them.

When to review written advance directives

Maybe you're hoping that all this effort is a once in a lifetime experience. It could be, but in the future, there may be practical as well as personal reasons that you want to change the documents you've just toiled over. Advance directives are written on paper—not cast in stone. Life is full of surprises and one or more of them may prompt you to alter your thinking about end-of-life issues, whether that means changing your proxy appointments or amending your care instructions.

Some folks review all legal paperwork once a year, which does not necessarily mean they change anything, it just means they look it over and make sure they don't need to. You may also want to adopt a regular schedule of reviewing your written directives on your birthday each year or every other year or every odd-numbered New Year's Day. Whatever works for you. If you use an online calendar, you can put a repeating reminder on it.

Knowing what you now know, let's consider events that may prompt you to review your advance directives:

- Landmark life events such as retirement, a milestone birthday or a move can dramatically affect our perspective on life and always warrants a full review of all legal documentation. The same is true for events in your proxy's life, if they affect his ability to act on your behalf. Oh, and keep an eye on your state's law for any changes that affect your documentation.

- When you experience a death or divorce at close range, it can influence your attitudes about end-of-life care decisions. If you lose your spouse/proxy or in-law/proxy to death or divorce, new advance directive forms are immediately in order.

- A change in your physical well-being can transform those imaginary health care scenarios into real-life probabilities. If you become seriously ill, talk to your proxy about any symptom-specific directives that may now be appropriate. When a proxy suffers a medical condition that affects his ability to make decisions on your behalf, consider whether you need to appointment someone else.

Revising and revoking written advance directives

General rule: written advance directives should be replaced and the old editions revoked if your choice of proxy or wishes for medical care or end-of-life care change. Before rushing to fill out a new form and rip up the old one, first check the language contained within your written advance directive to comply with any revocation procedure stated there. Also consult your state's law or legal counsel to see if there are formal statutory revocation requirements. It is almost never a good idea to <u>amend</u> legal documents such as advance directives because it usually results in a marked-up and initialed jumble that needs to be executed again in full to be valid. It's easier and safer to have replacement documents prepared. Once the new advance directive documents have been fully executed, witnessed and notarized—and not until—destroy any previous versions. Distribute new copies to all concerned parties, either collecting the replaced forms or requesting that they be shredded.

Chapter Review

- The Durable Power of Attorney for Health Care and Living Will forms you use must contain certain elements to qualify as complete and enforceable legal documents.
- An alternative to having the two traditional advance directive forms is a combination document that contains the appointment of a health care proxy and instructions to be carried out by the patient's physician and proxy.
- If you choose to hire an attorney to assist in the preparation of your written advance directives—which is highly recommended—the cost will be minimal if you do your homework before you arrive at the attorney's office.
- If you decide to go the do-it-yourself route, you'll find that many good forms are available for free or at a very minimal cost.
- In eight states, an advance directive form is mandated by state law. If you wish to embellish one of these state forms in any way, please seek legal counsel to avoid creating conflicts or confusion.
- There are many advance directive forms available, usually provided by nonprofit organizations. Preview several and find the one that is the best choice for your unique needs. The combination advance directive form Five Wishes® is inexpensive, straightforward and it does the job.
- Nothing in the HIPAA privacy rules affects the appointment of decision-making authority granted in a Durable Power of Attorney for Health Care.
- Once your written advance directives are fully signed, witnessed and notarized in compliance with your state's law, distribute copies and carefully store the rest.
- Where you keep your written advance directives is not as critical as who knows where that is. Be sure to tell your proxy and alternate proxy where they can find the originals of your advance directives and other important legal documents.
- You should review your advance directives whenever an event occurs that may affect their content. They should be replaced, revoking the previous versions, if your choice of proxy or wishes for medical care or end-of-life care change for any reason.

OMG. This is it. You really did it.

Or you're just about to. If having effective advance directives isn't an achievement worthy of a celebration, then what is? Once your written advance directives are signed, sealed and delivered, you will have accomplished what less than one third of adult Americans have gotten around to doing: having a real plan to maintain self-determination at the end of life by documenting thoughtful choices for medical and life prolonging care and appointing a qualified proxy decision maker. If you're somewhere in the process of getting all that done, give yourself a soft deadline to achieve each step and it will be behind you in no time.

Every bit as important as granting yourself peace of mind is giving your loved ones the blessing of being prepared to effectively manage your care if and when the time ever comes. Job well done.

Now get outta here and go live your life!

Forgive, O Lord, my little jokes on Thee,
And I'll forgive Thy great big one on me.
Robert Frost

Chapter Ten
The Ethical Will:
Your beliefs, wisdom and hopes

What you leave behind is not what is engraved in stone monuments,
but what is woven into the lives of others.
Pericles

Actually, there is one more thing I want to talk to you about. When I wrote the first edition of this book in 2006, I included a short chapter on a topic I had just learned about. Throughout the following six years, I became so obsessed with the subject of that one chapter and all it can mean that I wrote three more books devoted to it.[132] Indulge me while I tell you the story of how that came to be and why you should care . . .

A 20-year-old stands in front of the Chicago & Northwestern Railroad office in Boone, Iowa. Hat in hand, he takes a deep breath, stands tall to make the most of his scant six foot build and opens the heavy oak door.

In the midst of a national post-war depression, Boone boasts a remarkably large population of 12,800 for the year 1921, mostly owing to its primary industry of coal: mining it and moving it. America's railway system has just been returned to private ownership after years of wartime nationalization. That explains the trains, lots and lots of trains. This veteran of the First World War has come to apply for work as a railroad laborer. He is one of almost 4,000,000 "doughboys" returning to civilian life and desperate to find a job.

His name is James Harold Godfred Kline, my Uncle Bill. (His brother John was called Uncle Frank, Aunt Winifred was christened Susie and my father Eugene was known as Uncle Dutch. The Klines are big on nicknames.) Uncle Bill got that job, and after three years of advancing from laborer to baggageman to check clerk to yard clerk, he took a 15-month hiatus to attend Iowa State College (now Iowa State University) in Ames, Iowa and then returned to the railroad in December 1925 to resume his job as yard clerk. But that was just the beginning.

His career advanced in sync with the railroad industry: from Boone, Iowa to Clinton, Iowa to Madison, Wisconsin to Chicago, Illinois to Mason City, Iowa and ultimately to Marquette, Michigan in 1948. Thirty-one years after starting as a laborer in Boone, Iowa, J. H. "Bill" Kline was named President of the Lake Superior & Ishpeming Railroad Co. on the shores of the Great Lakes' largest, Superior. When I think of Uncle Bill and Aunt Isabel, I always think of their home and lifestyle in Marquette, Michigan.

Uncle Bill commanded a powerful presence. Obsessively hardworking and self-assured, he excelled as an industrial, political and civic leader. Aunt Isabel was the consummate homemaker and assumed the role of my uncle's partner in every sense with class and dignity. Looking back, I now realize the commitment it must have taken in the 1950s and 1960s to keep these two branches of the Kline family so close; we had many unforgettable visits with them in Iowa and Michigan.

They both passed away in 1977, Uncle Bill suddenly and Aunt Isabel following a few months later. I remember them well and lovingly, and their place as icons in the Kline family is secure. So when I became the custodian of their personal papers and photos in 2002, I eagerly dug in, knowing that I would be uncovering some truly amazing stuff. And I did.

First was a black and white photo of four suited gentlemen, obviously taken sometime in the 1950s. Yes, that is definitely Jimmy Stewart and Otto Preminger; I recognize Uncle Bill as the one on the far right. Then I remembered that the 1959 movie, Anatomy of a Murder, *was filmed on location in Marquette and the Upper Peninsula. I'd adore that movie even if my Uncle Bill hadn't been involved with it, but it's even more captivating because he was. I looked at the premiere dinner program autographed by every cast member and couldn't help but wonder what it might fetch on eBay.*

I've always been a political junkie, regardless of the ebb and flow of my party affiliation, and in this box of manila folders and brown clasp envelopes was a time capsule of old-fashioned politics, a wealth of American artifacts from the cold war 1950s and turbulent 1960s, complete with campaign buttons and chicken dinner menus. There was an autographed photo: "To Bill Kline with best wishes, Everett M. Dirksen, U.S. Senate." I recalled the Senator's famous quotation: "A million here, a million there. Pretty soon you're talking real money." Uncle Bill had saved an appreciative letter from President Eisenhower after a fundraising event. A 1960 telegram from failed presidential candidate Richard Nixon lay atop a transcript of Uncle Bill's congressional testimony on the jeopardized future of the American rail system. Extraordinary souvenirs were uncovered, one after another. I was, as we Iowans say, in hog heaven.

And then, among the invaluable ephemera representing a lifetime of public and professional service, I found the truly priceless treasure tucked away in that box.

At first glance, it looked just like any other letter. It was the 1960s—we wrote letters. We wrote letters when we went away to camp, to college, on vacation and every other week of the year. Communication options were limited: long distance phone calls were a luxury reserved for national holidays and the announcement of an unexpected death; e-mail was 40 years in the future. This was one of countless letters that had passed from one sibling to another, between my Uncle Bill and his brother, my father Eugene.

But this was not just like any other letter. It was written by my uncle on Thursday, March 28, 1963, one week before his retirement and four months after the death of his only child, Mary Kathryn. It was a letter my father had kept for 20 years until his own death in September 1982, stowed safely for me to find another 20 years later.[133]

Uncle Bill's letter included his insights on spirituality, his health regimen, the Serenity Prayer, tips on how to handle difficult people, a quotation from Voltaire and a bit of humor. It was composed on a Smith Corona portable typewriter in his home in Marquette, Michigan (I know that because it was typed on the back of a church bulletin). And my discovery of it forever changed my life.

About 3,500 years before Uncle Bill wrote that letter to my father, another fellow was the first to do something very similar. His name was Jacob and not long before his death, he shared with his twelve sons his reflections on some of the highlights (and low points) of life for him and them, lessons he had learned and his hopes for the future. You can read all about it in the first book of the Bible, Genesis.[134]

Fast forward to a few years after I found Uncle Bill's letter. I was privileged to volunteer with a hospice where I learned that dying patients were being encouraged to create their Ethical Wills, a record of their beliefs and values, life lessons and hopes for the future. It was meant to be an enduring legacy for their survivors, and it sometimes became a way for the patients and loved ones to express "Good bye" or "I love you."

Lightbulb moment! for me. Uncle Bill had created more than just a treasured family heirloom as he reflected on the values, lessons and hopes in his life. Like Jacob, Uncle Bill had left the permanent legacy of his Ethical Will.

History is replete with examples of Ethical Wills, from the Middle Ages to the Holocaust, from Anne Dudley Bradstreet's first poetry in The New World to Professor Randy Pausch's *Last Lecture*. It's not a legal document, it's so much more. An Ethical Will is the opportunity to be definitive about your life philosophy, the lessons you've learned in the school of hard knocks and what you hope the future will bring for you and for your loved ones.

This book on advance directives has been all about planning for life's end, but what then? No, I'm not talking about the afterlife. I'm referring to what happens to the people you leave behind once you're gone. How will they remember you and what you stood for? In their hearts and minds, what will your legacy be?

Two interesting studies by the folks at Allianz Life Insurance Company of North America concluded that the overwhelming majority of Baby Boomers and their parents consider values, life lessons and family stories the most important legacies to receive and pass on, respectively; more important than financial assets or real estate or the expectation of inheritance.[135] What? The most valuable legacy cannot be measured in dollars and cents? Didn't see that one coming.

Your Ethical Will, whether it's a letter or an elaborate PowerPoint slideshow or a beloved collection of quotations, can be more than just a treasured family heirloom to share while you're still here or even to be discovered after you're gone. A study posed this question to patients who had made serious care decisions for themselves and to proxies who had done the same on behalf of others: "What activities best prepared you for decision making?" The number one answer was "Identifying values based on past experiences and quality of life."[136] Life lessons and values. Not a medical prognosis or even an illuminating burden/benefit analysis. Life lessons and values.

Likewise, the exercise of thinking about what you believe, what you know and what you hope for can be the lodestar for your choice in heirs, health care proxies and even guardians for dependents. An Ethical Will can be the foundation for value-inspired philanthropy and for an estate plan that targets beneficiaries and charitable causes that affirm your ethical legacy. A permanent record of what you stand for is just that—permanent. I call it Footprint Philanthropy™. [137]

Consider learning more about the contemporary practice of this ancient tradition and making the creation of your Ethical Will part of your advance health care planning. Then share your ethical message with your legal and financial advisors and loved ones so they will better understand what you stand for and how you want to be remembered.

Lightbulb moment! Not sure what medium you'd like to use to express the message of your Ethical Will? In the meantime, create an "Ethical Will" file or 9x12 envelope. And don't stash it away—keep it where it's easily found. Anytime you run across a quotation, story, scripture, song, thought or life experience that you might want to include in your Ethical Will, toss it in there. Once you figure out how you're going to express your ethical message for your loved ones, you'll have a head start on its contents.

Chapter Eleven
The chapter where I tell you what I think
(read: fact-based rant)

Death is a very dull, dreary affair,
and my advice to you is to have nothing whatever to do with it.
W. Somerset Maugham

Whenever we witness someone—whether in person or courtesy of the mass media—whose wishes for end-of-life care are being disregarded, both our compassionate and apprehensive voices cry out, "That's just not right!" We want desperately to crusade for a way to stop that from ever happening again, especially since the victimized patient could be us sometime in the future.

Grasping for solutions, some have gone in search of the perfect form, like the default option Living Will, which I'm pleased to observe is falling out of favor. That's the one where a declarant states, "I want all life prolonging measures to be withheld, period." You know, the default option a few have decided is the preference of all. I'm not advocating for the indefinite prolonging of life, because I would agree that most people probably don't want that. But it's important to understand that when you turn advance health care planning into a deceptively simple "If A, then B" proposition, any further discussion (read: communication) is thwarted. If you agree that advance directives should be reflective of a person's beliefs, values, theology and life experience, then recognize that this is unlikely to be the outcome when expressed in a 120-word cookie-cutter document. The whole default option idea is pretty silly when you think about it. If never having life prolonging measures is everyone's preference, there is really no need for advance directives at all.

Along those same lines, since 1990 we've relied on the Patient Self-Determination Act to educate the public and health care professionals about the importance and meaning of advance directives. That's worked out well.

The POLST form was hailed as the solution to unavailable, misunderstood and disregarded advance directive forms not doing their job. Conspicuous by its absence over the past 24 years is any meaningful research on whether POLST orders are honored with more frequency than written advance directives. And, considering the individual states' freedom to tinker with some of the most significant features of the POLST paradigm (e.g., respect for the patient's existing advance directives, the obligation to obtain patient or proxy authorization, use restricted to those who are truly frail or terminally ill), I don't see how this improves the patient's lot. That's who we mean to be looking out for, right?

Waves high the hand of the next expert schmexpert in line, "I know! I know! The problem is we haven't digitized patient's preferences into standardized and accessible electronic records!" Does that mean health care professionals will be reading a copy of my advance directives on a laptop in the emergency room? Because I'm not convinced that a doctor skimming my Living Will on the fly will be a step in the right direction. Or is someone in the hospital admissions office going to read, interpret and then condense the qualitative essentials of my Living Will into three- or four-letter status codes for the attending physician to access on his smartphone?

From standardized forms it's a short leap to standardized dying.

Sure enough, here comes the "My grandmother died peacefully in her sleep. I'll have what she had." constituency. For that group, the way to address any potential pain and suffering at life's end is to have a doctor and pharmacist arrange for an early flight, thereby avoiding all the messy parts of dying. Death on demand. I'm all for patient autonomy but where physician-assisted suicide is concerned, is it death with dignity or expediency that is achieved? As a society, until we've done a much better job of raising public and professional awareness of palliative care options, should we be so quick to sanction prescriptions for suicide pills?

I don't know. I do know we're partial to one-size-fits-all solutions around here.

Like this one: We have a disgraceful shortage of organ and tissue donors. Come to think of it, though, I can't recall ever seeing a media campaign to encourage donor registration (oh, to have one organ transplant ad for every hair transplant ad). Nevertheless, there is now increasing interest in making organ donation a "presumed consent" system. The distinction is clear: under our existing method of explicit consent, the donor or his survivors must "opt in" to allow donation; under presumed consent, all persons are considered donors unless they "opt out." Hmm.

When I look at all the possible solutions being proffered, I haven't quite decided if each is intended to foster autonomy or merely uniformity. I do know this, for sure: those two objectives are mutually exclusive and I vote for autonomy.

As a coping mechanism, denial isn't working. If we stop to envision what must surely be just beyond the horizon, demographically speaking, we will completely freak out. Still, we need to do it. How are we going to deal with these issues logistically, financially, morally and spiritually over the next few decades as we encounter double the number of persons 65 and older and triple the number of those 85 and older?[138] What will constitute a practical yet compassionate approach when 80 percent of Medicare is now being spent on adults with more than four chronic conditions?[139]

There's a study being conducted right now in which some Medicare patients continue to receive curative treatment while also receiving palliative services. This is called "concurrent care," and in theory it will improve patient and family satisfaction and bring terminal patients into the hospice sphere earlier.[140] It's a potential game-changer in the use of hospice in this country and holds great promise, or it would, except that simultaneously, the 2010 Affordable Care Act included a $17 billion cut to hospice provider reimbursement over the ten years ending 2022. That's the same as chopping one year's funding from the decade. (By the way, hospice currently accounts for a whopping two to three percent of the annual Medicare budget.[141]) These cuts are not just digits in a federal budget—they are real patients being deprived of real services. While I'm on the subject of service providers, today we have a nationwide shortage of 7,500 full-time hospice and palliative care physicians[142] and the dangerous level of unfilled nursing jobs we are already experiencing is projected to number 526,800 by 2022 and 918,232 by 2030.[143] Yipes.

Did I mention the caregivers? Well, they deserve to be mentioned again. Twenty-nine percent of adult Americans are taking care of someone who is ill, disabled or aged.[144] We rely on that unseen, unrecognized and uncompensated army of workers in this country to maintain the caliber of health care we enjoy. An upside of the Baby Boom was having so many children in each family, but time is running out on that built-in convenience.

And we're not alone.

Canada's Supreme Court just ruled that its ban on physician-assisted suicide and the law against consenting to being killed (euthanasia) are both unconstitutional. It gave Canadian lawmakers one year to pass—or not pass—laws regulating both practices.[145] That's in a country where over half of the adults have never discussed their end-of-life wishes with anyone, and there is already a dramatic shortage of available palliative care resources.[146]

Why must death and dying fall into the ever-growing category of topics that compel each of us to plant our feet squarely in defense of an ideology? Let's have a conversation—the kind where each side listens and has the opportunity to explain and then learn from the other guy—as a society and as individuals. Because I don't think we need more forms or more laws, I think we need more conversations.

There was a huge kerfuffle over another provision of the Affordable Care Act. It would have reimbursed health care providers for taking the time to discuss end-of-life options with their patients. It was omitted from the enacted law, which is a shame, since we've known for some time that the major reasons people don't have advance directives is because they don't have the information they need to create them. And, oh yeah, nobody ever talked to them about it. At the same time, to even suggest that doctors refuse to discuss such matters with patients unless they are adequately compensated for doing so is wrongheaded. If, indeed, there is any hesitation on the part of health care professionals to talk about death and dying, I think it comes from the same place as for the rest of us: *Where do I start and what do I say once I get started?* And, of course, *Does the other person really want to hear this?*

And speaking of talking, feel free to do some of your own. Let's see if we can't get the participation rate of American adults with well-considered advance directives a lot higher than 28 percent. Ask your friends and family what they think about how we're addressing the issues surrounding health care and end-of-life care in this country. Now that you've read this book, you're likely to be the smartest person in the room.

We are long overdue for a meaningful public discourse on the social, emotional, spiritual and practical implications of death and dying in America, but that doesn't mean it's too late.

It's not too late.

For further information

State-specific information and forms

Try "health care directives [state name]" in any search engine to find your state's health department, attorney general or department on aging for information and forms.

Links to state bar associations – HG.org Legal Resources
http://www.hg.org/northam-bar.html

State Health Care Power of Attorney Statutes – Selected Characteristics – January 2013
American Bar Association Commission on Law and Aging
http://www.americanbar.org

Default Surrogate Consent Statutes as of June 2014 - ABA Comm. on Law and Aging
http://www.americanbar.org

Health Care Decision-Making Authority of
Health Care Agents vs. Court-Appointed Guardians
American Bar Association Commission on Law and Aging 2003
http://www.americanbar.org

Advance directive forms

Five Wishes® combination advance directive form – Aging With Dignity
http://www.agingwithdignity.org

Center for Practical Bioethics
http://www.practicalbioethics.org

National Resource Center on Psychiatric Advance Directives
http://www.nrc-pad.org/

National Alliance on Mental Illness
http://www.nami.org

"Dementia Provision" for advance directives - Compassion and Choices
https://www.compassionandchoices.org

Having The Big Talk with loved ones

Five Wishes® advance directive form – Aging With Dignity
(also free Presentation Guide and PowerPoint slideshow for groups)
http://www.agingwithdignity.org

Center for Practical Bioethics Caring Conversations booklet
http://www.practicalbioethics.org

The Conversation Project Starter Kit
http://www.theconversationproject.org

"let's have DINNER and talk about DEATH"
http://www.deathoverdinner.org

Communicating with health care professionals
Being Moral —Medicine and What Matters in the End
by Atul Gawande (ISBN 978-1-62779-055-0)

"A Physician's Guide to Talking About End-of-life Care"
by Richard B. Balaban, M.D.
(written for physicians but an excellent tool for both sides of the conversation)
http://www.ncbi.nlm.nih.gov

Out of Hospital - Do Not Resuscitate orders
Links to states' laws on OOH-DNRs – American Medical ID
http://www.americanmedical-id.com/extras/dnr.php

Physician Orders for Life Sustaining Treatment (POLST)
Regulatory/Legislative Comparison of State Programs – as of 2/15/2015
http://www.polst.org
(source: American Bar Association Commission on Law and Aging)

Physician-assisted suicide
Patients Rights Council
http://www.patientsrightscouncil.org/site/

Death With Dignity National Center
http://www.deathwithdignity.org/

Organ donation
Information and links to state organ donor registries
U.S. Dept. of Health and Human Services
http://www.organdonor.gov

Hospice and palliative care information
National Hospice and Palliative Care Organization
http://www.nhpco.org

Funeral or memorial planning
Links to information on planning alternatives - Funeral Consumers Alliance
http://www.funerals.org

"Shopping for Funeral Services" - Federal Trade Commission
http://www.consumer.ftc.gov

Recommended reading
Being Moral —Medicine and What Matters in the End by Atul Gawande

The Four Things That Matter Most – A Book About Living by Ira Byock, MD

tuesdays with Morrie by Mitch Albom

On Death and Dying by Elisabeth Kubler-Ross, MD

So Grows the Tree – Creating an Ethical Will by Jo Kline Cebuhar, JD

The Last Lecture by Randy Pausch with Jeffrey Zaslow

Endnotes

Chapter One – Denial isn't just a river in Egypt

1 "Hula Hoop," How Products are Made, Volume 6, www.madehow.com (accessed March 10, 2015).

2 U.S. Census Bureau, Statistical Abstract of the United States: 2003, Table HS-27. Housing Units—Historical Trends for Selected Characteristics: 1940 to 2000, www.census.gov.

3 U.S. Census Bureau, Historical Census of Housing Tables, Home Values, Median Homes Values, www.census.gov (accessed September 24, 2014).

4 U.S. Census Bureau, Historical National Population Estimates: July 1, 1900 to July 1, 1999, Revised date: June 28, 2000, www.census.gov.

5 Sandra L. Colby and Jennifer M. Ortman, "The Baby Boom Cohort in the United States: 2012 to 2060, Population Estimates and Projections," Current Population Reports, Issued May 2014, U. S. Department of Commerce, www.census.gov.

6 U.S. Census Bureau, Current Population Survey, Annual Social and Economic Supplement, 2012, Table 1. Population by Age and Sex: 2012, www.census.gov.

7 Center for Disease Control and Prevention, National Vital Statistics System, Mortality 2013, LCWK2. Deaths, percent of total deaths, and death rates for the 15 leading causes of death in 10-year age groups, by race and sex: United States, 2013, www.cdc.gov/nchs/nvss/mortality.

8 U.S. Census Bureau, 2012 Population Estimates and 2012 National Projections, Table 2. Projections and Distribution of the Total Population by Age for the United States: 2012 to 2050, www.census.gov.

9 Lindsay M. Howden and Julie A. Meyer, U.S. Census Bureau, Age and Sex Composition: 2010, 2010 Census Briefs, May 2011, www.census.gov.

10 Pew Research Center, "Baby Boomers Retire," December 29, 2010, www.pewresearch.org.

11 Pew Research Center, Religion & Public Life Project, "Views on End of Life Medical Treatments," November 21, 2013, www.pewforum.org.

12 Ibid.

13 Centers for Disease Control and Prevention, National Hospital Ambulatory Medical Care Survey, Table 2. Emergency department visits, by patient age, sex and residence: United States, 2010, www.cdc.gov.

14 Gerald F. Riley and James D. Lubitz, "Long-term Trends in Medicare Payments in the Last Year of Life," Health Services Research, Centers for Medicare and Medicaid Services, April 2010, www.hsr.org.

15 "End of Life Care, Inpatient days per decedent during the last six months of life, by gender and level of care intensity: Year 2012," The Dartmouth Atlas of Health Care, www.dartmouthatlas.org (accessed February 15, 2015).

16 Centers for Disease Control and Prevention, National Center for Health Statistics, Health, United States, 2010: With Special Feature on Death and Dying, Data table for Figure 33. Place of death, over time: United States, 1989, 1997 and 2007, www.cdc.gov/nchs.

17 U.S. Department of Health and Human Services, Administration on Aging, "A Profile of Older Americans: 2011," www.aoa.gov.

18 Jaya K. Rao, MD et al., "Completion of Advance Directives Among U.S. Consumers," American Journal of Preventive Medicine, Volume 46, Number 1, January 2014, www.ajpmonline.org; HealthDay/Harris Poll, November 12-17, 2014, www.harrisinteractive.com.

19 Pew Research Center, Religion & Public Life Project, "Views on End of Life Medical Treatments," November 21, 2013, www.pewforum.org.

[20] Jason Fields and Lynne M. Casper, "America's Families and Living Arrangements, March 2000," Current Population Reports, U.S. Census Bureau, www.census.gov.

[21] U.S. Census Bureau, American Community Survey, 2011, Table 1. Households by Type and Selected Characteristics: ACS 2011, www.census.gov.

[22] Centers for Disease Control and Prevention, Health, United States, 2013, Table 3. Crude birth rates, fertility rates and birth rates, by age, race, and Hispanic origin of mother: United States, selected years 1950-2012, www.cdc.gov.

[23] U.S. Department of Health and Human Services, Administration on Aging, "A Profile of Older Americans: 2011," www.aoa.gov.

[24] Jaya K. Rao, MD et al., "Completion of Advance Directives Among U.S. Consumers," American Journal of Preventive Medicine, Volume 46, Number 1, January 2014, www.ajpmonline.org; Liora Adler and Heather Sered, "Advance Directives in Family Practice," Einstein Quarterly Journal of Biology and Medicine, Volume 18, 2001.

Chapter Two – The Living Will: Instructions for your care and feeding

[25] U.S. Department of Health and Human Services, Administration on Aging, "A Profile of Older Americans: 2011," www.aoa.gov; U.S. Census Bureau, 2012 Population Estimates and 2012 National Projections, Table 2. Projections and Distribution of the Total Population by Age for the United States: 2012 to 2050, www.census.gov.

[26] U.S. Department of Health and Human Services, Administration on Aging, A Statistical Profile of Older Americans Aged 65+, August 27, 2003, www.aoa.gov.

[27] Centers for Disease Control and Prevention, National Vital Statistics Report (NVSR) "Deaths: Final Data for 2013," Table 7. Life expectancy at selected ages, by race, Hispanic origin, race for non-Hispanic population, and sex: United States, 2013, www.cdc.gov/nchs.

[28] Monroe Lerner, *When, Why and Where People Die* (New York: Russell Sage Foundation, 1970).

[29] Ian Dowbiggin, *A Merciful End: The Euthanasia Movement in Modern America* (New York: Oxford University Press, 2003).

[30] Ibid.

[31] Julia Quinlan interview by Barbara Manieri, Sparta Independent, January 6, 2000, www.karenannquinlanhospice.org.

[32] In the Matter of Karen Quinlan, an Alleged Incompetent, The Supreme Court of New Jersey, 70 N.J. 10 (1976), 355 A. 2nd 647 (1976).

[33] Cruzan v. Harmon, The Missouri Supreme Court, 760 S.W. 2d 408 (Mo. 1988).

[34] Cruzan, By Her Parents and Co-Guardians Cruzan et ux. v. Director, Missouri Department of Health, et al., 497 U.S. 261 (1990).

[35] William H. Colby, *A Long Goodbye* (Carlsbad, California: Hay House, Inc., 2002).

[36] Omnibus Budget Reconciliation Act of 1990, P. L. 101-508, sec. 4206 and 4751, 104 Stat. 1388, 1388-115, and 1388-204 [classified respectively as 42 U.S.C. 1395cc(f) (Medicare) and 1396a(w) (Medicaid), commonly referred to as The Patient Self-Determination Act].

[37] In Re: The Guardianship of Theresa Marie Schiavo, In the Circuit Court for Pinellas County, Florida, Probate Division, File No. 90-2908GD-003, February 11, 2000.

[38] Title XLIV, Chapter 765, Sections 205, 305 and 401, Florida Statutes.

[39] In re: Guardianship of Theresa Marie Schiavo - Robert Schindler and Mary Schindler v. Michael Schiavo, as Guardian of the person of Theresa Marie Schiavo, In the District Court of Appeal of Florida Second District, Case No. 2D02-5394, June 6, 2003.

[40] Kathy Cerminara and Kenneth Goodman, University of Miami Ethics Programs, "Key Events in the Case of Theresa Marie Schiavo," www.miami.edu (accessed October 6, 2014).

[41] In Re: The Guardianship of Theresa Marie Schiavo, In the Circuit Court for Pinellas County, Florida, Probate Division, File No. 90-2908GD-003, February 11, 2000.

[42] Maria J. Silveira, MD, MPH et al., "Advance Directives and Outcomes of Surrogate Decision Making Before Death," The New England Journal of Medicine, Volume 362, No. 13, April 1, 2010, www.nejm.org.

[43] Ibid.

[44] Scott D. Halpern et al., "The Care Span - Default Options in Advance Directives Influence How Patients Set Goals for End-of-life Care," Project HOPE, Health Affairs, Volume 32, No. 2, February 2013, www.healthaffairs.org.

Chapter Three – The Durable Power of Attorney for Health Care

[45] In the Matter of Karen Quinlan, an Alleged Incompetent, The Supreme Court of New Jersey, 70 N.J. 10 (1976), 355 A. 2nd 647 (1976).

[46] Pamela B. Teaster, PhD et al., "Wards of the State: A National Study of Public Guardianship," March 31, 2005, American Bar Association Commission on Law and Aging, www.americanbar.org (accessed December 19, 2014).

[47] "Guardianship for the Elderly: Protecting the Rights and Welfare of Seniors With Reduced Capacity," Issued by Senator Gordon H. Smith, Ranking Member, United States Senate Special Committee on Aging and Senator Herb Kohl, Chairman, United States Senate Special Committee on Aging, December 2007.

[48] "About the National Certified Guardian Exams," National Guardianship Association, Inc., www.guardianship.org (accessed December 19, 2014).

[49] National Resource Center on Psychiatric Advance Directives, www.nrc-pad.org (accessed December 19, 2014); "Psychiatric Advance Directives: An Overview," National Alliance on Mental Illness, www.nami.org (accessed December 19, 2014).

[50] "Population Clock," U.S. Census Bureau, www.census.gov (accessed December 19, 2014).

[51] U.S. Pet Ownership & Demographics Sourcebook (2012), American Veterinary Medical Association, www.avma.org.

Chapter Four–The key to effective advance directives: Your proxy is your voice

[52] "Who has the right to make decisions about your funeral?" Funeral Consumers Alliance™, December 2, 2013, www.funerals.org.

[53] In the Matter of Karen Quinlan, an Alleged Incompetent, The Supreme Court of New Jersey, 70 N.J. 10 (1076), 355 A. 2nd 647 (1976); "Opinion 8.081 – Surrogate Decision Making," AMA Code of Medical Ethics, American Medical Association, www.ama-assn.org (accessed December 17, 2014).

[54] Mi-Kyong Song, "Disconnect between emergency contacts and surrogate decision-makers in the absence of advance directives," Palliative Medicine, Volume 27, Number 8, February 1, 2013, www.pmj.sagepub.com.

[55] "Civil Unions & Domestic Partnership Statutes" and "Same-sex Marriage Laws," National Conference of State Legislatures, www.ncsl.org (accessed January 6, 2015).

[56] "Default Surrogate Consent Statutes as of June 2014," American Bar Association Commission on Law and Aging, www.americanbar.org.

Chapter Five – So little time, so much to choose from

[57] Steven Laureys, "Death, unconsciousness and the brain," Nature Review/Neuroscience, Volume 6, November 2005; The Multi-Society Task Force on PVS, "Medical Aspects of the Persistent Vegetative State," The New England Journal of Medicine, Volume 330, No. 21, May 1994.

[58] "What is dementia?" and "2014 Alzheimer's Disease Facts and Figures," Alzheimer's Association, www.alz.org (accessed January 8, 2015).

[59] Center for Disease Control and Prevention, National Vital Statistics, Mortality 2013, LCWK2. Deaths, percent of total deaths, and death rates for the 15 leading causes of death in 10-year age groups, by race and sex: United States, 2013, www.cdc.gov/nchs/nvss/mortality.

[60] Ibid.

[61] Margaret Ann Bentley v. Maplewood Seniors Care Society et al., In the Supreme Court of British Columbia, 2014 BCSC 165, February 3, 2014; Margaret Anne Bentley, Appellants, v. Maplewood Seniors Care Society, Respondents, 2015 BCCA 91, March 3, 2015.

[62] "AMA Policy on Provision of Life-Sustaining Medical Treatment," AMA Code of Medical Ethics, The American Medical Association, www.ama-assn.org (accessed December 15, 2014); American Medical Association Code of Medical Ethics, "Opinions on Social Policies," "Opinion 2.20 – Withholding or Withdrawing Life-Sustaining Medical Treatment," www.ama-assn.org (accessed January 8, 2015).

[63] Cruzan, By Her Parents and Co-Guardians Cruzan et ux. v. Director, Missouri Department of Health, et al., 497 U.S. 261 (1990).

[64] R.A. Berg et al., "Part 5: Adult Basic Life Support – 2010 American Heart Association Guidelines for Cardiopulmonary Resuscitation and Emergency Cardiovascular Care," Circulation, Volume 122, Issue 18, Suppl 3, November 2, 2010, www circ.ahajournals.org.

[65] "CPR Statistics," American Heart Association, www.heart.org (accessed January 19, 2015).

[66] Myke S. van Gijn, MS et al., "The chance of survival and the functional outcome after in-hospital cardiopulmonary resuscitation in older people: a systematic review," Age and Ageing, Oxford Journals, Volume 43, Number 4, July 2014, www.ageing.oxfordjournals.org.

[67] Tae J. Lee, MD, CMD and Kathryn M. Kolasa, PhD, RD, LDN, "Feeding the Person With Late-Stage Alzheimer's Disease," Nutrition Today, Volume 46, Number 2, March/April 2011; American Geriatric Society Ethics Committee and Clinical Practice and Models of Care Committee, "American Geriatrics Society Feeding Tubes in Advance Dementia Position Statement," Journal of American Geriatrics Society, Volume 62, No. 8, August 2014, www.AmericanGeriatrics.org.

[68] "Treatment Methods for Kidney Failure: Hemodialysis," National Kidney and Urologic Diseases Information Clearinghouse, A service of the National Institute of Diabetes and Digestive and Kidney Diseases, National Institutes of Health, www.kidney.niddk.nih.gov (accessed January 20, 2015); "Dialysis: Deciding to Stop," National Kidney Foundation, www.kidney.org (accessed January 20, 2015).

[69] L. M. Cohen et al., "Practical considerations in dialysis withdrawal: 'To have that option is a blessing'," Journal of the American Medical Association, Volume 289, No. 16, April 2003.

[70] "Implantable Cardioverter Defibrillator (ICD)," American Heart Association, www.heart.org (accessed January 20, 2015).

[71] Daniel Fischberg, MD, PhD et al., "Five Things Physicians and Patients Should Question in Hospice and Palliative Medicine," Journal of Pain and Symptom Management, Volume 45, No. 3, March 2013; Rachel J. Lampert, MD, FACC, "Death Does Not Have to Be a Shocking Experience: Deactivation of Cardiac Rhythm Devices at Patients' End of Life," American College of Cardiology, August 29, 2012, www.acc.org.

[72] Jessica Schuster, MD et al., "Hospice Providers Awareness of the Benefits and Availability of Single-Fraction Palliative Radiotherapy," Journal of Hospice & Palliative Nursing, Volume 16, Number 2, April 2014.

[73] "Opinion 2.201 – Sedation to Unconsciousness in End of life Care," AMA Code of Medical Ethics, American Medical Association, www.ama-assn.org (accessed January 21, 2015).

[74] Richard M. Doerflinger and Carlos F. Gomez, MD, PhD, "Killing the Pain Not the Patient: Palliative Care vs. Assisted Suicide," United States Conference of Catholic Bishops, www.usccb.org (accessed January 21, 2015); Nicholas J. Kockler, MS, PhD, "The Principal of Double Effect and Proportionate Reason," American Medical Association, Virtual Mentor, www.virtualmentor.ama-assn.org (accessed January 20, 2015); "HPNA Position Statement – The Ethics of Opioid Use at End of Life," Hospice and Palliative Nurses Association, www.hpna.org (accessed January 15, 2015).

[75] Michaela Bercovitch, MD and Abraham Adunsky, MD, "Patterns of High dose Morphine Use in a Home-Care Hospice Service," National Cancer Institute at the National Institutes of Health, June 2004, American Cancer Society, www.cancer.org; N. Sykes and A. Thorns, "The use of opioids and sedatives at the end of life," The Lancet, Oncology, May 2003; A. Thorns and N. Sykes, "Opioid use in last week of life and implications for end of life decision-making," The Lancet, July 2000; Michaela Bercovitch, MD et al., "High dose morphine use in the hospice setting - A database survey of patient characteristics and effect on life expectancy," National Cancer Institute at the National Institutes of Health, September 1999.

[76] "Great-grandma tattoos 'DO NOT RESUSCITATE' on her chest," Des Moines Register, May 16, 2006 and Jo Kline Cebuhar, JD, "Iowa View: Tattoos alone won't guarantee medical wishes," Des Moines Register, June 4, 2006.

[77] "Opinion 2.22 – Do-Not-Resuscitate Orders," AMA Code of Medical Ethics, American Medical Association, www.ama-assn.org; "Guidelines for the Appropriate Use of Do-Not-Resuscitate Orders," Journal of the American Medical Association, Volume 265, No. 14, April 1991.

[78] Ferdinando L. Mirarchi, DO et al., TRIAD (The Realistic Interpretation of Advance Directives) studies, "Triad III: Nationwide Assessment of Living Wills and Do Not Resuscitate Orders," The Journal of Emergency Medicine, Volume 42, No. 5, May 2012.

[79] Charles P. Sabatino, American Bar Association Commission on Law and Aging and Naomi Karp, AARP Public Policy Institute, "Improving Advanced Illness Care: The Evolution of State POLST Programs," AARP Public Policy Institute, April 2011, www.aarp.org/ppi.

[80] "POLST and Advance Directives" and "About the National POLST Paradigm," The National POLST Paradigm, www.polst.org (accessed January 26, 2015).

[81] Charles P. Sabatino, American Bar Association Commission on Law and Aging and Naomi Karp, AARP Public Policy Institute, "Improving Advanced Illness Care: The Evolution of State POLST Programs," AARP Public Policy Institute, April 2011, www.aarp.org/ppi.

[82] In sixteen "endorsed" or "mature" states 1) the POLST-type form overrides previous advance directives, 2) priority is given to the form most recently executed or 3) the issue of document priority is not addressed ["POLST Program Legislative Comparison – as of 2/15/2015," www.polst.org (prepared by the American Bar Association Commission on Law and Aging)]. The NPPTF site states that "Only patients with serious illness or frailty, for whom a health care professional would not be surprised if they died within one year, should have a POLST form." Nevertheless, various NPPTF "mature" and "endorsed" POLST state programs include persons with an incurable injury, anyone admitted to a nursing facility, someone with a serious health condition and those with up to five years' life expectancy. [Colorado, Hawaii, Idaho, Indiana, Minnesota, New Jersey, Nevada]. In

reference to patient authorization, some states do not require patient or proxy execution of the POLST form even though formal acknowledgement is evidence of the physician's fulfillment of a duty to provide information to his patient, as well as of the patient's informed consent ["POLST Program Legislative Comparison – as of 2/15/2015," www.polst.org (prepared by American Bar Association Commission on Law and Aging) and the American Medical Association Code of Medical Ethics, "Opinion 8.08 – Informed Consent," www.ama-assn.org].

[83] Russell Contreras, "New Mexico appeals court to hear assisted suicide case," The Associated Press, January 23, 2015.

[84] "State-by-State Guide to Physician-Assisted Suicide," Euthanasia Pros and Cons, www.euthanasia.procon.org (accessed January 27, 2015).

[85] Russell Contreras, "New Mexico appeals court to hear assisted suicide case," The Associated Press, January 23, 2015.

[86] Vacco v. Quill, 521 U.S. 793 (1997) and Washington v. Glucksberg, 521 U.S. 702 (1997).

[87] "William J. Clinton, XLII President of the United States, 1993-2001, Statement on Signing the Assisted Suicide Funding Restriction Act of 1997," The American Presidency Project, www.presidency.ucsb.edu (accessed January 27, 2015).

[88] Oregon's Death with Dignity Act annual reports, 1997-2013, The Oregon Public Health Division, www.public.health.oregon.gov (accessed January 26, 2015).

[89] Washington State Department of Health Death with Dignity Act annual reports, 2009-2013, Washington State Department of Health, www.doh.wa.gov (accessed January 26, 2015).

[90] "Death-With-Dignity Boom: 26 States Now Considering Laws," Compassion & Choices, www.compassionandchoices.org (accessed February 18, 2015).

[91] "Chronology of Dr. Jack Kevorkian's Life and Assisted Suicide Campaign," Frontline®, The Public Broadcasting System, www.pbs.org (accessed January 27, 2015).

[92] Keith Schneider, "Dr. Jack Kevorkian Dies at 83; A Doctor Who Helped End Lives," The New York Times, June 3, 2011, www.nytimes.com.

[93] "State-by-State Guide to Physician-Assisted Suicide," Euthanasia Pros and Cons, www.euthanasia.procon.org (accessed January 27, 2015).

[94] U. S. Department of Health & Human Services, "Organ Procurement and Transplantation Network," www.optn.transplant.hrsa.gov (accessed February 10, 2015).

[95] U.S. Government Information on Organ and Tissue Donation and Transplantation, U.S. Department of Health & Human Services, Donate the Gift of Life, "Timeline of Historical Events / Significant Milestones in Organ Donation and Transplantation," www.organdonor.gov (accessed February 10, 2015).

[96] "Opinion 2.157 – Organ Donation After Cardiac Death," AMA Code of Medical Ethics, The American Medical Association, www.ama-assn.org (accessed February 10, 2015).

[97] "Controversies in the Determination of Death," The President's Council on Bioethics, January 2009.

[98] U.S. Government Information on Organ and Tissue Donation and Transplantation, U.S. Department of Health & Human Services, "State Organ Donation Legislation," www.organdonor.gov/legislation_micro (accessed February 10, 2015).

[99] In re: The estate of Mary Florence Whalen, Deceased, Michael Whalen, Appellant (2013), www.caselaw.findlaw.com/ia-supreme-court/1624122.html.

[100] Pew Research Center, Religion & Public Life Project, "Views on End of life Medical Treatments," November 21, 2013, www.pewforum.org.

[101] "Opinion 2.037 – Medical futility in End-of-life Care," AMA Code of Medical Ethics, American Medical Association, www.ama-assn.org (accessed February 12, 2015).

Chapter Six - Hospice and palliative Care

102 "A Short History," Hospice Education Institute, www.hospiceworld.org (accessed December 1, 2014).

103 NHPCO Facts and Figures: Hospice Care in America 2014 Edition, National Hospice and Palliative Care Organization, October 2014, www.NHPCO.org.

104 "How hospice works," The Centers for Medicare and Medicaid Services, www.Medicare.gov (accessed December 1, 2014).

105 H. Swerissen and S. Duckett, "Dying Well," Grattan Institute Report No. 2014-10, September 2014, www.grattan.edu.au.

106 NHPCO Facts and Figures: Hospice Care in America 2014 Edition, National Hospice and Palliative Care Organization, October 2014, www.NHPCO.org.

107 Kevin Ache, DO et al., "Are Advance Directives Associated with Better Hospice Care?," Journal of the American Geriatrics Society, Volume 62, Issue 6, June 2014, www.geriatricscareonline.org.

108 Margaret Jean Hall, PhD et al., "Trends in Inpatient Hospital Deaths: National Hospital Discharge Survey, 2000-2010," U.S. Department of Health and Human Services, March 2013, www.cdc.gov/nchs.

109 NHPCO Facts and Figures: Hospice Care in America 2014 Edition, National Hospice and Palliative Care Organization, October 2014, www.NHPCO.org; U.S. Department of Health and Human Services, Centers for Disease Control and Prevention, National Center for Health Statistics Data Brief No. 178, December 2014, "Mortality in the United States, 2013," www.cdc.gov/nchs.

110 Shelley I. White-Means, and Zhiyong Dong, "Valuing the Costs of Family Caregiving: Time and Motion Survey Estimates," Consumer Interests Annual, Volume 58, 2012, www.consumerinterests.org.

111 NHPCO Facts and Figures: Hospice Care in America 2014 Edition, National Hospice and Palliative Care Organization, October 2014, www.NHPCO.org.

112 Ibid.

113 "Choosing a Quality Hospice for You or Your Loved Ones," National Hospice and Palliative Care Organization, www.HNPCO.org (accessed March 14, 2015).

114 NHPCO Facts and Figures: Hospice Care in America 2014 Edition, National Hospice and Palliative Care Organization, October 2014, www.NHPCO.org.

115 "How hospice works," The Centers for Medicare and Medicaid Services, www.Medicare.gov (accessed December 1, 2014).

116 NHPCO Facts and Figures: Hospice Care in America 2014 Edition, National Hospice and Palliative Care Organization, October 2014, www.NHPCO.org.

Chapter Seven - Communicating with loved ones and health care professionals

117 "Understanding Life Support Measures," The Cleveland Clinic, www.clevelandclinic.org (accessed February 25, 2015).

118 Proceedings of the National Medical Conventions, held in New York, May 1846 and in Philadelphia, May 1847, originally published by T.K. & P.G. Collins, 1847, www.ama.nmtvault.com.

119 Atul Gawande, *Being Mortal – Medicine and What Matters in the End* (New York: Metropolitan Books – Henry Holt and Company, LLC, 2014); Ezekiel J. Emanuel and Linda L. Emanuel, "Four models of the physician-patient relationship," The Journal of the American Medical Association, Volume 267, Number 16, April 22, 1992.

120 Ferdinando Mirarchi, DO, FAAEM, FACEP, "A New Nationwide Patient Safety Concern Related to Living Wills, DNR Orders, and POLST-Like Documents," National

Patient Safety Foundation, "Patient Safety Blog," www.npsf.org (accessed February 24, 2015); Robert Glatter, MD and Ferdinando L. Mirarchi, DO, "Advance Directives May Be Hazardous to Your Health," Medscape Internal Medicine, www.medscape.com (accessed January 22, 2015).

[121] In the Matter of Karen Quinlan, an Alleged Incompetent, The Supreme Court of New Jersey, 70 N.J. 10 (1976), 355 A. 2nd 647 (1976).

[122] Atul Gawande, *Being Mortal – Medicine and What Matters in the End* (New York: Metropolitan Books – Henry Holt and Company, LLC, 2014).

Chapter Eight – The "what-ifs" of advance directives

[123] Pew Research Center, Religion & Public Life Project, "Views on End of life Medical Treatments," November 21, 2013, www.pewforum.org.

[124] Ibid.

[125] Charles P. Sabatino, "De-Balkanizing State Advance Directive Law," American Bar Association Commission on Law and Aging, BIFOCAL, Volume 25, No. 1, Fall 2003.

[126] Lesley S. Castillo, BA et al., "Lost in Translation: The Unintended Consequences of Advance Directive Law on Clinical Care [Table 2]," Annals of Internal Medicine, Volume 154, No. 2, January 18, 2011.

[127] Jan Slater, "Oklahoma's Remarkable Laws Regulating End of Life," Oklahoma Bar Association, Oklahoma Bar Journal, Volume 85, No. 26, October 4, 2014; "Information for Patients and Their Families, Your Medical Treatment Rights Under Oklahoma Law," Oklahoma Medical Board, www.okmedicalboard.org (accessed February 17, 2015).

Chapter Nine – Putting it all together with written advance directives

[128] "Aging with Dignity Five Wishes States," Aging with Dignity, www.agingwithdignity.org (accessed February 27, 2015).

[129] "Five Wishes®" form dated June 2011, Witness Statement declarations, Aging With Dignity, www.agingwithdignity.org.

[130] Laura M. Kressel et al., "The Influence of Default Options on the Expression of End-of-life Treatment Preferences in Advance Directives," Journal of General Internal Medicine, 2007; Scott D. Halpern et al., "Default Options in Advance Directives Influence How Patients Set Goals for End-of-life Care," Health Affairs, Volume 32, No. 2, February 2013; "Dying in America: Improving Quality and Honoring Individual Preferences Near the End of Life," Institute of Medicine of the National Academies, September 17, 2014.

[131] U.S. Department of Health & Human Services, Health Information Privacy FAQ, www.hhs.gov (accessed December 18, 2014).

Chapter Ten - The Ethical Will: Your beliefs, wisdom and hopes

[132] Jo Kline Cebuhar, JD, *SO GROWS THE TREE – Creating an Ethical Will* (West Des Moines, Iowa: Murphy Publishing, LLC, 2010), *The Workshop Edition of SO GROWS THE TREE* (West Des Moines, Iowa: Murphy Publishing, LLC, 2011) and *Whose big idea was that? Lessons in giving from the pioneers of value-inspired philanthropy* (West Des Moines, Iowa: Murphy Publishing, LLC, 2012).

[133] Ibid.

[134] God et al., Genesis 49, The Holy Bible.

[135] The Allianz American Legacies Study, conducted in 2005 by The Allianz Life Insurance Company of North America in collaboration with Dr. Ken Dychtwald of Age Wave, www.allianzlife.com; The Allianz American Legacies Pulse Study, conducted in January 2012

by The Allianz Life Insurance Company of North America, May 23, 2012, press release at www.allianzlife.com.

[136] Ryan D. McMahan, BS, BA et al., "Advance Care Planning Beyond Advance Directives: Perspectives From Patients and Surrogates," Journal of Pain and Symptom Management, Volume 46, Issue 3, September 2013.

[137] Jo Kline Cebuhar, JD, *Whose big idea was that? Lessons in giving from the pioneers of value-inspired philanthropy* (West Des Moines, Iowa: Murphy Publishing, LLC, 2012).

Chapter Eleven – The chapter where I tell you what I think (read: fact-based rant)

[138] U.S. Census Bureau, Population Division, Table 2. Projections of the Population by Selected Age Groups and Sex for the United States: 2015 to 2060, Release Date: December 2012, www.census.gov.

[139] "2014 Policy Priorities," The American Geriatrics Society, www.AmericanGeriatrics.org (accessed January 4, 2015).

[140] "Medicare Care Choices Model," Centers for Medicare & Medicaid Services, www.innovation.cms.gov (accessed December 2, 2014).

[141] "The Affordable Care Act," U.S. Department of Health and Human Services, www.hhs.gov/budget/ (accessed October 9, 2014); "Medicare and Changes Under Affordable Care Act (ACA) – AARP," AARP, www.aarp.org (accessed October 9, 2014).

[142] D. Lupu, "Estimate of current hospice and palliative medicine physician workforce shortage," Journal of Pain and Symptom Management, Volume 40, Number 6 (2010).

[143] Bureau of Labor Statistics, "Economic News Release," Table 8. Occupations with the largest projected number of job openings due to growth and replacement needs, 2012 and projected 2022, www.bls.gov (accessed March 27, 2015); Stephen P. Juraschek, BA et al., "United States Registered Nurse Workforce Report Card and Shortage Forecast," American Journal of Medical Quality, Volume 27, No. 3, January 2012.

[144] "Caregiving in the U.S. 2009," National Alliance for Caregiving in Collaboration with AARP, 2009, www.caregiving.org (accessed October 15, 2014).

[145] Carter v. Canada (Attorney General), Supreme Court of Canada , 2015 SCC 15, February 6, 2015.

[146] Sheryl Uberlacker, "Palliative care crisis looming for Canadians nearing end of life, report says," The Canadian Press, December 15, 2014, www.ctvnews.ca.

About the author

Attorney Jo Kline Cebuhar's books on end-of-life legal and health care issues and the meaning of legacy include the award-winning **Last things first, just in case . . . The practical guide to Living Wills and Durable Powers of Attorney for Health Care** and **SO GROWS THE TREE – Creating an Ethical Will**. Jo's first novel **EXIT**, set in a small-town hospice, was released in 2014. Her writing has been featured in *The New York Times*, *Reader's Digest*, *The Philadelphia Inquirer* and *The Des Moines Register*. Jo formerly served as chair of Iowa's largest hospice and lives in West Des Moines, Iowa.

Jo's email: JoKlineCebuhar@msn.com

www.JoKlineCebuhar.com

www.Advance-Directives.net

CPSIA information can be obtained
at www.ICGtesting.com
Printed in the USA
LVOW03s1616190716
496926LV00011B/174/P